LEADERSHIP INTERRUPTED

DAILY INSPIRATION TO BECOME THE LEADER YOU WERE MEANT TO BE

Kevin DeShazo

Praise for Leadership Interrupted

"*Leadership Interrupted* is full of practical, powerful insights to help you become a better leader-no matter what your title is. The great news is you can start today!"
Jon Gordon, best-selling author of *The Power of Positive Leadership*

"You're too busy to not read this book. It will give you the courage to lead and create and connect with what truly matters. Don't miss it."
Jeff Goins, best-selling author of *The Art of Work*

"These messages are a part of my morning routine, challenging me to be the best leader I can be. They set the tone for my day and provide me with an opportunity to reflect on our culture and how my actions as a leader effect it."

Brad Folkstead, Associate Athletic Director for Communication and Marketing, Bemidji State University

"This book is for everyone who works in an organization, from top to bottom. Leadership Interrupted gives you a day-by-day approach to being a better leader at work, at home and in your everyday life."

Gary Paczesny, Director of Digital Media at University of Memphis Athletics

"Leadership Interrupted" is a must-read every morning. It helps me be a more prepared and better leader, no matter what team I am working with."

Rob Carolla, Director of Communications, College Football 150th Anniversary

CoSIDA President, 2017-18

"It is the first thing I read at my desk each morning. It always makes me think and helps to set my day with the right emphasis."

Andrew Carter, Director of Athletics at Minot State University

"This daily reminder has helped me to lead where I am, keep moving forward to do the difficult work and has led to me making a positive impact on my team and department."

Jessica Harbison Weaver, Associate AD for Compliance and Academic Support/ Senior Woman Administrator

Concordia University, Portland

To my wife, Megan, who not only puts up with the crazy ideas and dreams that come into my brain, but for supporting them, for leading our family, for fiercely loving our boys and me, for being you. Every day is better because of you.

To my friends and community and family who put up with me, support me, love me, laugh with (and at) me and make me better, my life is richer because of you. Let's keep growing old together while refusing to believe that we're growing old.

To Jeremie Kubicek, Steve Cockram and the GiANT Worldwide family, you guys mean the world to me. This wouldn't have been possible without you. It's an honor to run the race with you.

To my boys, this is all for you. I'd try to add more words here but it's hard to see the screen through tears. I love you like crazy.

Introduction

You're busy. Your calendar is filled with meetings and to-do lists and projects and more meetings. You received 10 new emails while reading this. And you have soccer practice and meet the teacher night and a dozen other things.

You want to be a great leader but you don't know how to take the first step and you feel like you don't have enough time. Good news? You can be that leader and you do have the time. In this book you will get daily inspiration, often in less than five minutes, to challenge your thinking, reshape your perspective and call you up to be a leader worth following at the office and at home. Is this book for the CEO and the head coach? Yes. But it's also for the sales manager, the HR coordinator, the receptionist, the new grad, the maintenance crew. Leadership is for everyone.

Back in 2014 I started sending a daily email to challenge and inspire leaders in athletics. Having traveled the country working with college athletes, coaches and administrators, I realized there was a gap in leadership development. That email grew to partnering with GiANT Worldwide and creating Culture Wins Championships, where we've worked with hundreds of leaders and teams to help them become better leaders and teammates who build championship culture. This book is 365 of the more than 1300 daily emails I've sent.

We've seen leaders be transformed, teams that were on life support come alive and cellar dwellers become championship winners. Hearts have changed, teams have changed, families have changed, lives have changed. I'm excited for your story to be added to the list.

365 days in the year. 365 days of inspiration and challenge in this book. If you don't want to become a great leader, go back to your inbox. If you do, get started. I'd love to hear your progress and thoughts and encourage you along the way, so don't hesitate to reach out to me on

Twitter (@kevindeshazo), call/text me at 405.535.6943, or email at deshazo.kevin@gmail.com

Your journey to becoming one of the best leaders in the world starts today. Let's get started.

Cheers

Kevin

Table of Contents

Daily Inspiration

Day 1

Depending on which study you look at, the average person spends more than 2.5 hours per day worrying about money. That's nearly a month and a half per year lost to worry. And that doesn't include time worrying about our jobs, families and health. We're constantly battling questions of worry. *Am I good enough? What if I don't get the promotion? What if this project fails and my boss stops believing in me and I get fired? What if my team stops trusting me? What if, What if, What if?*

Nothing kills joy faster than worry. Nothing destroys your ability to lead faster than worry. Worry forces you to think small and takes your mind off the task at hand. It impacts your relationships and your health. Worry causes you to lead from a place of fear and it results in you not trusting others or yourself. Nothing positive comes from worry. The reality is that worrying won't change or prevent anything. Life still happens.

The nice thing about worry is that **you** control it. You can wake up in the morning and *trust* in your abilities. *Trust* in your team. *Trust* in the work that you are doing. *Trust* in the vision. Trust leads to empowering others, creativity, and boldness. Trust brings joy. And let's be honest, we can all use a bit more joy.

So what will you choose today? Will you choose worry, or will you choose to trust?

Day 2

We live in a world of criticism. Everybody's a critic, an expert in exposing your flaws. Open up your Twitter or Facebook account (for you, your team or your department) and odds are you'll find no shortage of haters. Critics love their own voices. They love to rattle you, to get you to respond, to alter your course. Critics don't want to help you or make you better. They want to stop you from working. Critics hate work.

If we're not careful we can become consumed by our critics. It's natural to want to prove doubters wrong. But you have a job to do. A team to lead. People to serve. Family to love. You know your purpose and your plan. You already know your strengths and weaknesses. You know the facts that critics can't know and don't care to know. So you can focus on your critics or you can focus on your work. On moving forward. On creating.

Anyone can be a critic. Only the courageous create.

Day 3

Don was the COO of a large healthcare company I used to work for. Don was known as the most encouraging and positive man in the company. He made every person feel valued, regardless of position or how long they had been with the company. Spend five minutes with him and your confidence went through the roof. His secret? His mindset.

Don realized early on in his career that his attitude was the key to his day. Like all of us, his days were filled with ups and downs. Successes and failures. He knew the only thing he could control was how he responded. He knew that to be an effective leader, to get the most out of every day and out of every employee, he had to master his mind.

He decided that he wouldn't enter the office until he was in the right mindset. He would sit in his car in the parking lot for as long as it took to get mentally ready, a practice he modeled for more than 30 years. Some days he was ready as soon as he pulled into the lot, while other days it might take 30 minutes. It became a running joke in the company that you don't bother Don when he's giving himself a parking lot pep talk. Under Don's leadership and encouragement, the company saw more than a decade of record growth and landed as high as No. 3 on the Forbes "100 Best Companies to Work For" list - a personal project of his.

Your team is relying on you to be at your best. To inject positivity, confidence and vision - in good times and bad. You can't do that when you walk in distracted and anxious about the day ahead.

Before you walk through the doors, spend some time to get your mind right.

Day 4

Director or Influencer.

Directors give orders, push forward without listening to others and avoid interaction. Have a relationship with those they lead? Directors view that as a sign of weakness.

Influencers cast vision, they listen to what's happening around them and adjust as necessary. Influencers are dialed in to the heartbeat of their team, knowing what makes each person tick.

Directors worry about changing the bottom line. Influencers worry about impacting people. Which will you be today?

Day 5

When was the last time you were challenged at your job? Not had a long, exhausting day or a difficult meeting but really, truly challenged. A moment or day that stretched you beyond your abilities, that made you think, "Maybe I'm not as good as I thought." It could be a day that you failed. When you first started out, odds are many days were like this. You were enthusiastic, wanted to prove yourself and would do whatever it took, without fear of failure. You simply knew you would do whatever it took to figure it out. Over time we tend to settle into our positions and routines. We feel confident in our skills, decisions and vision. Every day looks similar to the one before. We stop learning.

We have a tendency to settle for safe. Safe is easy and familiar. If we're honest, we think the safe route makes us look smarter to others - when earlier on it was risk and willingness to try anything that got us noticed. Most of all, safe is boring. A result of safe we often overlook is that we're passing it down to our teams. We're building teams that don't face challenges. Teams that don't dream big dreams. Teams that don't learn from failure because they don't try anything at which they might fail at. Teams that don't look or function like actual teams.

Have the courage to take on projects that stretch you, that cause you to question your skills. Work that makes you nervous and uncomfortable. Encourage your teams do to the same, and remove the fear of failure. Embrace the adversity that comes from a challenge, and harness that into a powerful moment for you and your team.

Day 6

Some of us naturally lack confidence. Others go through seasons where our confidence just isn't there. Then there are times where we're so busy that we forget who we are and where we're going. It's not a confidence issue, it's a purpose issue.

Do you have a mission and identity statement? That may sound weird, but it's a statement declaring who you are (identity), what you're about (values) and what you're doing (your purpose). Go big with it. This is one of the things I start my day with. It's not as much of a pep talk as it is a reminder.

There are days when this statement is a boost of confidence and there are day where it's simply my compass, re-centering me on what matters. There are seasons where I'll read it at times during the day as well.

The world will throw a lot at us trying to distract us from what matters and trying to get us to believe lies about ourselves. If we lose sight of who we are, we lose our ability to lead well and accomplish our mission.

Start each day with a reminder of who you are and where you're going. Make a habit of calling yourself up to who you were meant to be.

Day 7

You've been entrusted to lead a group of men and women. To guide them, to cast vision. To correct them and inspire them.

But how are you leading you? Do you approach your days with discipline and purpose or are you living each day as if it's just the next in a line of many?

Love and serve your team, but don't become so focused on others that you neglect to lead yourself.

Day 8

We're always looking for better ways to accomplish tasks. Too often, we think better means faster. With our busy schedules, we focus on efficiency. Faster isn't necessarily better. Sure you can take a short-cut and maybe nobody will notice, but you have to live with your work. Your name, your reputation, your legacy is attached to your work and the work of your team.

Your work is your craft. You are a craftsman (or craftswoman). In Jon Gordon's book *The Carpenter*, he has this to say about a craftsman:

"A craftsman is an artist who builds a work of art. While most people approach their work with the mindset that they just want to get it done, a craftsman is more concerned with who they are becoming and what they are creating rather than how fast they finish it."

Take pride in your work, in your art. It's more than just another task to complete.

Day 9

Everybody wants to be successful. We work for it, dream about it, stress over it. We want our campaigns to be effective, our projects to work and our teams to win. Once success is achieved, we celebrate. We rightfully pat ourselves and our teams on the back and relish the moment.

But do you plan for what comes after success? How do you respond and move forward? Too often we ride the high of success and, before we know it, we're in the midst of a new set of problems — problems that might have been avoided had we thought about our next move. Don't just enjoy the mountaintop. Be grateful for the moment but know exactly what got you there and how you can maintain it. Know what your next move will be. Plan for tomorrow.

Success isn't easy. The real challenge is to be prepared for what comes next.

Day 10

You are in the business of building people. While that seems obvious enough, too often we operate out of the mindset that our mission is to build a business, grow a department, strengthen a brand. Without our people, we have no business to build, team to grow, brand to strengthen. Your success is their success.

Your team members are a reflection of you. Are they disorganized, stressed, just getting by, or are they focused, energized, and prepared? Are they just doing their work, or are they embracing the mission of the organization?

Make time for those on your team. Time where they have 100% of your attention. Time to listen to them individually and collectively. Time to thank and acknowledge them. Time to dream with them.

People are the heartbeat of any organization and team. Put people first.

Day 11

John was my boss for several years. One day while waiting to get his tires rotated, he started a conversation with the man next to him in the customer lounge. After discovering the man was a dialysis patient at a nearby clinic, John asked about his nurses and the care they provided. "I'm alive because of my nurses. I owe them everything." John returned to the office and shared this story with his sales team - a team responsible for generating more than $40 million per year in profit. "We aren't just making calls, making placements (sales), staffing clinics. We're saving lives. The work we're doing matters. These patients need us." This team, mired in the monotony of making more than 100 sales calls per day to hit a number of budgetary and organizational goals, had found its why.

It's easy to get lost in your daily routine of tasks, forgetting (or worse, not knowing) the real purpose of your work. Do you know who is impacted by your decisions? Who feels the effect of the work you do? Do you know the reason you get up and come into work every morning? Not money, title, status - the *real* reason.

Do you know your why? More importantly, does your team know it?

Day 12

What's it like to work for you? Are you cultivating an environment of positivity? Is your department a place where people are challenged, encouraged, striving for greatness? Does your team know that you are for it? Does everyone have clear goals and expectations? Or are you absent, shut off and inconsistent?

If you were your boss, would you want to work for you?

The ultimate test of leadership is this: What is life like for those under your authority?

Day 13

The greatest strategy in the world won't work if you don't have the right culture. If those on your team are not behind you, knowing what they are working for and why, your plans and ideas will never get off the ground. Sure, they'll perform their tasks but only because it is their job. They won't work with passion, won't strive for greatness, won't work *for* you. They will simply follow orders. You are not leading an assembly line. You are leading a team, a family.

Culture is greater than strategy. Build the right team, create the right culture, then develop and implement your strategy.

Day 14

Leaders are not motivators. They realize they cannot give someone a reason to perform a task, to do great work, to go the extra mile. Motivators try to get people excited about something they don't truly want to do. Motivation is vocal persuasion. True leaders are influencers. Their work, values, attitude and commitment cause others to act. They inspire from within. Influencers don't need to hold a pep rally to get their teams excited.

Influencers infect others with purpose. They live on a mission and draw others into it. Influencers are worth following.

Day 15

Part of your job as a leader is to know when to let others take over. To let others on your team use their strengths and gifts to move the project forward. To empower and encourage them to run the show. For some, this won't come naturally. You have fought your way to the top, honed your skills and earned your position. To let somebody else lead, even temporarily, feels like weakness.

Only, you didn't get to your position alone. At some point, somebody gave you the chance to lead. A leader stepped aside and gave you the floor for a moment, allowing you to flourish and grow.

Don't hold people back. Give away your platform. Look for greatness in your team and allow each of them to own it.

Day 16

Being a leader is a privilege, an honor. Leaders are tasked with casting vision for a group of people, sometimes for an entire organization. Leaders are given the opportunity to push, cheer, pull and guide a team through a variety of experiences. Leaders get to pick people up when they are down, help nothing become something, breathe life into a cause, to use their influence for the good of others.

Be aware and present for the moments that only leaders get to experience. Find ways to create more of those moments.

Day 17

It's natural to be anxious, especially at the beginning and during the middle of a project or season. You may even start to doubt yourself. Are you going the right direction, making the correct decision? Are you even the right person for the job?

Stop and look back. Look at how far you have come, at what you and your team have accomplished. Be thankful for the trials, the failures, the successes, the growth. Be thankful for each moment along the way that made you better. That allowed you to see things with the right perspective. That produced wisdom.

Thankfulness builds trust. Trust in yourself, your decisions and your team. Be thankful for where you've been, and trust where you are headed.

Day 18

How do you define success? One of the biggest struggles for a leaders, on both a personal and team level, is realizing when they've been successful. You always feel like you can do more, achieve more, work more. You are never satisfied. It is an exhausting way to live and work and prevents us from truly being happy. Without a specific definition of success you can't truly evaluate and grow. You never know where you are on the road.

Of course, success doesn't mean you are done. It doesn't mean you kick back and relax. You celebrate it, learn from it, then set out to achieve a new set of well-defined goals.

Day 19

When was the last time your perspective or direction was challenged? If we aren't careful, we get to a point where we operate in an environment that never challenges how we think. We surround ourselves with people who think the same way we do and chart a course that nobody ever questions. That's a dangerous place to be.

Read books and articles that offer a different view of the world. Follow people on Twitter who share different opinions than yours. You may change your mind, or you may solidify your positions. As leaders, it is vital that we know why we believe what we believe and why we do what we do. We can't do that if we shield ourselves from those we disagree with.

Day 20

Where are you today? For most leaders, we're always thinking about where we are going. We dream big dreams and are always looking ahead at what could be. We see the mountain in the distance and can't wait to get to the top. But you can't get to where you want to be if you don't know where you are. You'll never reach the mountain because you keep stumbling over the rocks on the road that leads to it.

Look around and take stock of where you are today. Of what is happening in the here and now. What needs your attention today, at this moment? You have to focus on getting to the mountain before you can think about climbing it.

Day 21

Whom are you serving? Check your heart and examine your motives. Are you making decisions to benefit you, looking for ways to advance your career? Or are you looking to help others succeed? Are you doing whatever is needed or do you believe that you are better than your job? Think of leaders you respect and aspire to be. Odds are high that they will tell you how great the people they lead are before they ever mention their own skills.

Great leaders know that what's best for their team is best for them. Great leaders are *for* their team. All the leadership skills in the world don't matter if your heart isn't right.

Day 22

What do you want to be known for? Are you about accolades or are you about people? When all is said and done, will people remember you only for the work you did or for the way you treated people? When people talk about John Wooden they acknowledge his success as a coach - it's impossible not to - but they focus on how he treated his players. Each one of them knew he mattered to Coach Wooden.

At the end of our days, what we accomplished won't matter. Awards, promotions and success are certainly not bad things, but whether you get those or not, you still have people you interact with every day. People who need encouraged, inspired, to have their voice heard. People worth investing in. Be about them.

Day 23

What big problem were you frustrated with or stressed out about yesterday? You know which one I'm talking about. The one that caused you to toss and turn in your bed, that consumed your thoughts regardless of the task you were working on. Can you even recall what it was? What about the problem from last week, last month, three months ago?

We tend to give our problems more value than they deserve. Too many times we treat problems and decisions as though they will make or break us when in reality we won't remember them in a few days. They are rarely as big and bad as we make them out to be.

Don't empower your problems. Give them the attention they deserve and nothing more, then move forward with a clear mind.

Day 24

You may be trapped by one of two things: the past or the future. You've made mistakes in your career. You've failed, screwed up, let somebody down. You are living out of those failures. Out of shame. Letting your past define who you are today.

"What if this project fails?" "They'll fire me, my colleagues will lose respect for me, my spouse will leave me and I'll never get hired again." Anxiety over the future may be filling your thoughts. Fear of what might happen is impacting how you view today.

You may even be trapped by both the past and the future. Living with both the shame of your mistakes and believing the failures that doomed your past are certain to repeat themselves and ruin your future.

You are enslaved by unhealthy thoughts. The truth is that you can't have unhealthy thoughts when you focus on the present. You are not your failures and you are not what might be. You are not who you were five years ago, five months ago, five days ago. You are not who you might be five days, months, weeks from now. You are you, today. Created to be you, in this moment.

Define yourself by what you do today. Don't be trapped by yesterday or tomorrow.

Day 25

Passion is arguably the foundation of success. If you aren't passionate about what you do, why are you doing it? Passion breeds energy, enthusiasm and positivity. That positivity is contagious.

Researchers at the University of Minnesota and Michigan State University conducted four separate studies of participants, to measure charisma, positive emotions and mood contagion. What they found was positive emotions are contagious. "Positive leaders were perceived as more effective and therefore more likely to persuade their followers" to do what they want them to do. This isn't about manipulation; it's about having a passion for what you do. Negative leaders had a negative impact on participants.

Maybe your team is in a rut, isn't responding, isn't excited about the work it's doing. If that's the case, examine yourself. Your team is a reflection of you.

Remind yourself of why you do what you do. Renew your passion and energy. Embrace your work with positivity and watch it spread. Be the catalyst for change.

Day 26

Do you know who you are? Are you confident in that? Leaders must be comfortable and confident in who they are. In their strengths and limitations. You can't find your value in the combination of your performance and the opinion of others. You can't *need* the respect of your team. You can't *need* the approval of your boss. You can't *need* for this project, campaign or season to be a success. Whether your team respects you, your boss believes in you or your project succeeds, you are still you. Would it be nice to have those things? Of course. Is it bad to want those things? Absolutely not. But they shouldn't be a prerequisite to happiness or self-worth.

There is a popular phrase in marriage counseling, where they tell couples to love more, need less. To truly be happy you have to love more, need *nothing*. When you need something from someone, you will constantly manipulate them in order to get what you need. Know you who you are and why you are.

Love more, need nothing. Be worth following.

Day 27

Are you better today than you were yesterday? What about a year ago? As leaders, we typically challenge our teams to push for more. We thrive on creating moments of discomfort because we know it leads to growth. That it will make them better. Lost in our desire to see others grow is our own development.

Constantly evaluate yourself. Find challenges each day that force you to rethink things, to examine your perspective and your skills. Don't get comfortable. Don't settle. That's when you start to lose your passion.

Every day is an opportunity to learn and grow. Don't neglect your own development.

Day 28

Be like Mike. We all remember the Gatorade commercial. If you were a kid growing up who loved sports, it was almost impossible to not want to be like Mike. He was a gamer, a winner, a champion. He delivered in the clutch. But why?

Do you remember the 1999 Nike commercial with Jordan?

"I've missed more than 9,000 shots in my career. I've lost almost 300 games. 26 times I've been trusted to take the game-winning shot...and missed."

Those are not exactly numbers we would associate with a winner. Jordan continues in that commercial, "I've failed over and over again in my life. And that is why I succeed."

Failure can crush us, or it can refine us. It can leave us defeated, or it can lead to greatness. How you respond to failure shows whether you are a pretender or a contender.

The good news? You get to decide how you respond.

Day 29

Consistency is a key attribute of a leader. Look at leaders you admire, both in your life and throughout history. One trait that flows through most, if not all, is consistency. Consistency got them to the top and consistency kept them at the top.

Consistency isn't easy. Our natural tendency, once we get to to the top, is to change who we are and how we operate. We eventually lose our identity and begin operating out of the expectations of others rather than out of our own confidence. We lose credibility and effectiveness, oftentimes forgetting what it is like to be in the shoes of those we now lead.

Remind yourself of what got you here. That attitude, those characteristics are what made you a success and staying true to them will keep you there.

Day 30

Every now and then we'll have one of *those* days. Every decision will seem to be the wrong one, nothing will go the way you expected or wanted, every light is red, every conversation is tense. Days that make you wonder if you're really qualified to be a leader, if you have what it takes, if you're on the right path. There are times when, instead of days, this feels like an entire season. Fear and resistance will tell you to quit. To give up. To throw your hands up and admit defeat.

It is during these days and these seasons that you must show up. Faithfully, and with renewed determination, show up. Commit to not being your own worst enemy. Do not be distracted.

Failure won't deter you, resistance won't overcome you, fear won't define you.

Day 31

Words are powerful. They inspire and they crush. They heal and they destroy. They encourage and they discipline. As a leader, this is even truer. Your words sit differently with others. They mean more, they hit harder, they carry farther.

No words are more important than those you speak to yourself. Those words determine how you speak to those you lead. If you are beating yourself up, tearing yourself down, labeling yourself a failure, you will push that negativity onto your team and your family. If you think positive thoughts about yourself, words that breed confidence, energy and passion, your team and family will reflect those.

Pay careful attention to the words you say to and about yourself. Think positive and you'll be positive. Think success and you'll be success.

Day 32

You can't be everything to everyone. Read that again. As many times as it takes for that truth to sink in. You cannot be everything to everyone. You can only be you. Embrace your strengths, and find freedom in your limitations.

You can't be everything to everyone, but what you can be is available. You can be present. And sometimes, that's really all that is needed.

Day 33

Do you have the same routine every day? Get up at the same time, leave the house at the same time, drive the same route to work, listen to the same radio station, drive the same route back home, listening to the same station. When was the last time you changed it up, took certain parts of your day off of auto-pilot?

Find ways to change your routine several times per week. Use these times to take note of the life going on around you, the stories that are being played out that you drive by every day without noticing. You'll gain new perspective, get your creative juices flowing.

Life is happening all around us. We just have to look up every now and then to see it. The more you're aware of it, the more you'll be inspired by it.

Day 34

Look in the mirror. You've likely just discovered the biggest hindrance to your leadership and effectiveness. It's you. You set the tone for your team. You lay out the vision for your department. You make decisions and take actions that impact how everyone else operates.

You must set the example. If you want greatness, be great. If you want success for your team, do the things that make all of you successful. If you want them to have a passion for what they do, show passion for what you do. Talk the talk and walk the walk.

Leadership begins with you. Be as great as you expect others to be.

Day 35

How do you respond when somebody questions your idea or plan? Do you get defensive? Do you assume they are out to get you, humiliate you, maybe take your job? Do you take it as a personal attack?

How much would it change things if, instead, you believed that people had the best of intentions? Sure, people aren't perfect, but ultimately your team is for you. Wouldn't it change everything if you really believed that? That in their mistakes, in their questions, in their challenging of your ideas that they simply want the team - which includes you - to succeed?

Let go of self-preservation. Remove yourself from the ownership of your ideas and believe that everybody on the team wants what is best for the team. It's not them versus you. It's them with you.

Day 36

We all battle doubts and fear. It could be about a project, a big meeting, speaking to a group, or it could be about the ability to do your job on a daily basis. Every day is a battle of replacing doubt with confidence. Overcoming fear with belief. Of replacing negative thoughts with positive.

But it isn't just you that faces this battle. Everybody you encounter is also facing fear. People on your team, in your department, those you interact with every day. How can you increase their confidence and stir up belief in them?

As you battle your own fear and doubt, look for ways to speak life and courage into those around you. Replace their negative thoughts with your positive words.

Day 37

Are you dominating people or are you liberating them? Dominators manipulate and push their own agenda, always looking out for themselves. They ignore the needs, strengths and weaknesses of others. The answer is always to work harder and work longer. They create a culture of fear and hesitation.

Liberators challenge others but make sure that the necessary support is there. They find their success in the triumphs of their team. They create a culture of passion, energy, creativity and success.

While dominators promote fear, liberators create movements. They bring about greatness in others. Which will you be today?

Day 38

You're leading people, but who is leading you? Who is guiding you, encouraging you, challenging you?

Great leaders always have somebody they respect. Someone who has the authority to tell them no. You can't pour into others if nobody is pouring into you. You can't effectively lead others if you're not being led.

Day 39

All eyes are on you. Every decision you make, word you speak, hire you make, play you call, direction you go is scrutinized. People are looking to you as not only their guide, but as a model of what to do themselves. Many of them want to be in your position, and they are learning what leadership looks like from you.

Hold yourself to a high standard. Realize the weight and impact that you have with your words and actions. You have the opportunity to shape lives, to influence future leaders. Be intentional in the example you set.

Day 40

Fear will tell you that nobody will like your idea. Fear will tell you that a co-worker will resent you making a suggestion that will actually make her better at their job. Fear will tell you to keep quiet in the meeting. That you don't even belong in that meeting. Fear will tell you to keep with the status quo. You've got a good thing going; why take a chance at messing that up? Fear loves boring.

Without change, we don't grow. Without change, nothing great happens. Without change, we get comfortable and lazy. Nobody wins. Except fear.

By all means, speak up. Step up. Stand out. We need you to. We're waiting for you to.

Day 41

Leadership isn't loud. It doesn't demand its way without regard for others. It isn't about accolades and recognition. It does not hold people back. It is not about the individual. It is not restricting.

Leadership is steady. It is consistent. It is about the greater good. It builds up. It serves. It works behind the scenes. It moves others forward. It empowers.

Leadership is often the opposite of how the world views it.

Day 42

Study after study reveals that an overwhelming majority of people are unhappy in their jobs. They sacrifice their own happiness for the sake of being "responsible" - providing for their families, paying the bills, etc. The most interesting thing is that they don't need a new job to make them happy. They can be happy just where they are.

That comes from you. Acknowledge your team. Value the team as people, not as numbers. Put them first. If you trust them, they'll return that trust with passionate work. If you value them, they'll come to work with purpose every day.

Don't manage and dictate them. Lead and inspire them.

Day 43

At some point in your career you will face challenges, maybe even threats. You could be experiencing that right now. Our natural tendency is to push that tension and fear onto our team, and retreat inwardly. We hole up in our office, cut off communication and hunker down for battle.

Self-preservation not only kills you, but it kills your team. Without a unified front, you make yourself vulnerable to more challenges and threats than the one you are currently facing.

This is not how we were meant to fight. This is not how leaders and teams and organizations survive. We were meant to fight our battles together, with our tribe. As a unit, goals clear, everybody working together for the team.

When those on your team feel like they belong, like they are trusted and included, then you can have a unified front that will conquer any challenge.

Day 44

Opportunity won't magically appear. Opportunity doesn't know how good your ideas are or how much of an impact you could make. It isn't concerned with your planning, your catchy slogan or your big dreams.

Opportunity is about one thing. Action.

You manufacture your opportunity. You make the opportunity, then you take advantage of it. You run with it and make that dream, that vision, that project a reality. But you have to start.

Opportunity is ready and waiting. Don't let somebody else take it. Show up today.

Day 45

Having a full calendar is not a sign of influence. Filling your day with meetings, conference calls, networking events and convention is not a badge of importance or status. It might mean you are ignoring your team.

Look through your schedule. Are the people on your team anywhere on it? Do you have times where you sit and talk with them? More importantly, do you have time scheduled to simply listen to your team? When are you learning about the challenges they are facing and what encouragement/direction they need from you?

Don't be "too busy" whenever those on your team need you. They are your priority. Your calendar should reflect that.

Day 46

Did you make it better?

At the end of each day, look back at the choices you've made. Remember each situation and conversation. You make hundreds of decisions each day, major and minor. You have countless interactions with employees, colleagues, clients, friends and family.

Did you make things better with your decisions? With your interactions? Is your team better for having come to work for/with you today? Is that client better off because of how you chose to treat/deal with him? Is your family better off for the way you chose to be present with them? Will your company be better if you hire/fire that person?

Decisions don't have to be as difficult as we make them out to be. Many times, it simply comes down to doing what will make things better. Commit to making things better.

Day 47

Are you OK with mediocrity? Worded that way, it sounds ridiculous. Of course you're not OK with it. When we think of mediocrity we think of words like boring, vanilla, ineffective, uninteresting.

Mediocrity doesn't win. It doesn't make things better. It doesn't change people, teams, organizations, the world.

Now look around you. Are you encouraging mediocrity with your words, your work, the way you lead? Are you unknowingly clinging to the status quo?

Be bold today. Be different. Reject mediocrity. Embrace opportunity.

Day 48

You and your team are part of a story. Every project, every game, every campaign adds to that story. You will have drama, comedy, tragedy, adventure, obstacles to overcome, victories. While new chapters will be written, it is a story that doesn't end.

When you realize you are living a story, you gain a new perspective. You understand you are a part of something bigger. You see problems as opportunities. Laughter unites. Failures lead to redemption. Victories are moments to fully experience. Employees are characters to develop and bring to life.

Open your eyes to the story you and your team are writing. Do your part to make sure it is a story worth telling.

Day 49

Sometimes as a leader, you don't know the impact you are having on people. That can be a difficult and frustrating thing, if you allow it to be. The truth is, that's what leadership is.

You show up every day. You do what you believe is right. You try to help others be better and believe in themselves. You suffer, rejoice, fail and succeed. You give of yourself for the sake of others. You can't measure those things. You can't put them in an annual review or financial report.

True influence is immeasurable. Be OK with that.

Day 50

Think about each person on your team or in your department. People that you interact with every day. People that you lead. Are you celebrating them or tolerating them? Are they celebrating or tolerating you?

People want to stay where they are celebrated. They want to know they are appreciated and valued, not merely tolerated. The same is true of leaders. You can't be effective if your team is simply tolerating you. If you are leading them well, they will fight for and celebrate you.

Great teams and organizations are made up of people who celebrate each other. Create an environment of celebration.

Day 51

What kind of atmosphere are you promoting around your team and organization? Are you cultivating hope, or are you pushing fear? When your employees, team, coworkers come in on Monday morning are they excited about the possibilities and potential of the weak, or are they already defeated?

Teams that are filled with hope are teams that pursue success, that sacrifice for one another and strive for greatness. Fearful teams are selfish and satisfied with just getting the job done.

Create a culture of hope. It starts with you.

Day 52

You are not a leader if you don't have people to lead. While that certainly isn't breaking news, many leaders tend to forget that they wouldn't be in leadership without someone following them.

People chose to follow you. They chose to work for you. They chose to have you lead them. They chose to be on your team. Even if they were there when you became their leader, they chose to stay. They put their trust in you.

That is a powerful and humbling reality. It should give you confidence and convict you to be purposeful with your words and actions. It should stir up appreciation.

Effective leaders are grateful. Don't ever stop thanking, encouraging and serving those who chose you as their leader. You wouldn't be here without them.

Day 53

What do you want to accomplish today? What are your goals? It's easy for us to have a big picture idea of what we want to do, of projects we want to complete, but what will you do today to move forward? What can make today a success?

Daily goals also help us move through times of frustration and difficulty. When you are in the midst of down season, you crawl your way out of it by accomplishing small, daily wins. These impact our mindset, empowering us to press on with renewed confidence.

Small, daily wins move us toward long-term success. How can you win today?

Day 54

It isn't fun to talk about, but sometimes leaders get stuck. You don't have the answer, you don't have the right words to inspire your team, you don't have an idea on how to move forward. As much as it may feel like it, that isn't a reflection of your ability to lead. It is simply reality.

Though people look to you for guidance, you are human. You won't always be on. The best way to get unstuck? Just as a writer overcomes writer's block by writing, a leader overcomes by consistently showing up. We don't run, we don't hide, we don't avoid. We show up.

Great leaders don't always have the answers, but they always show up. Be present, do the work, fight the battle.

Day 55

You can't control how your team responds. You can't control how your fans or clients behave. You don't know if this campaign will work, that project will fail, this hire will work out. So many variables are beyond your control. Leaders, unfortunately, love control.

What can you control? Your thoughts and your attitude. Fill your mind with positive thoughts. Positive thoughts lead to positive actions and words. Don't allow negativity to creep into your mind and your team. Negativity leads to doubt and division.

Give up worrying about things you can't control. Focus on your thoughts and your attitude. Those are up to you.

Day 56

Here in Oklahoma City, we had more than 25,000 people run in the 2014 Oklahoma City Memorial Marathon. They had prepared for months, gotten out of bed at 4:00 in the morning and headed to the starting line. Then weather hit and the start was delayed 15 minutes. Then 30. Then an hour. The race eventually started, 2 hours and 15 minutes after it was scheduled to begin.

Hours later, runners would cross the finish line. Some in under three hours, while others battled for more than 10 hours. They fought cramps, heat, exhaustion, and numerous other physical battles. Equally as daunting was the mental challenge. "Can I make it past this corner? Can I get over this hill? Can I make it another mile? Can I finish? I can't. I have to. I can. I will." They fought, they battled, they finished.

Leadership is a lot like a marathon. It never starts off the way you expected it to. You're going to face battles every mile. Every block. Your mental toughness will be challenged to its very core. Physically, it can take a toll on you.

But every step is a success. Every forward movement gets you closer to your goal. A thousand small victories move you toward the finish line. It's not about the time it takes, it's about not giving up along the way. It's about accepting and overcoming challenges, physical and mental. It's about believing in yourself.

Don't worry about the finish. Worry about conquering your next step. Believe you have what it takes to do it.

Day 57

What do you do when you are challenged? When your opinion suddenly goes against the grain? When it would be easier for you to change sides? You find out what you are made of then.

Do you give in and go with the flow, or do you hold your position? Do you go with what is convenient, or do you stand firm in your convictions?

If it hasn't yet, your stance will be challenged. Those who agreed with you will be on the other, suddenly more popular side. Followers will follow.

Leaders don't change for convenience. They don't ignore what they know to be right. They face adversity with truth and consistency. They do what leaders do. They lead.

Day 58

What are you building? A following, or more leaders? If you are building a following, you are making it all about you. You want people to serve you and be like you. You don't want them to learn and grow. You want to be their idol.

Leaders build more leaders. They serve, inspire and train people to lead. To follow their dreams, to create a new path, to challenge the status quo.

Gathering followers is the best way to lose sight of who you are and what you are about. You want make a difference? Build leaders. Then, when and if they leave, do it again. And again. And again. That's how you create a legacy that matters.

Day 59

How do you lead outside of work? That can be a weird question to think about. We spend a significant majority of our lives at work and, as a result, focus most of our development efforts in that area. We want to lead our team better, ourselves better (at work), our departments and companies better. We work to make a difference in the lives of those we interact with and find ways to develop them into leaders.

If we're not careful, we can neglect to develop ourselves outside of the office. We need to be equally focused on being better leaders with our family, our spouse and kids. Our community. The reality is that our experiences in one area will impact how we lead in other roles. It makes us a more effective and complete leader.

We can't pour everything we have into our career. A well-rounded leader impacts more than just the office.

Day 60

Weekends are not to be wasted by crashing. The temptation is to turn our brain off and check out. To go through the motions of a weekend without engaging, thinking this is a way to relax.

Your weekends should be a time that refuels you for the week. A time that energizes you, fills you up and gets you ready. Rather than check out, do something that actually gives you energy. Be with family, do yard work, go for a run, be with friends, work on that hobby you never have time for.

Weekends should prepare us for the week. Resist the urge to check out and find ways to renew your passion and purpose.

Day 61

Did you wake up today with a sense of expectation, or fear? Are you facing the morning excited about the opportunities that lie ahead, or are you already defeated, carrying the failures from yesterday, last week, last month or last year with you?

You aren't the same as you were last week. You aren't the same as you were yesterday. Today is a new day. A new opportunity to make a difference. Another chance to get better, to move forward, to make an impact on those around you.

Don't let fear and worry steal your day. Embrace each day with anticipation and purpose.

Day 62

When you listen, what are you listening for? Are you listening to reply or are you listening to understand? Great leaders are great communicators. Great communicators are effective listeners. They listen to understand, then they react accordingly.

Too often we "listen" while formulating our response. We don't care to understand the other person's position; we want to impose our perspective on them. Conversations become debates, and then battles. We lose the ability to connect with our team because we are too busy pushing our own agenda.

Take time today to listen. Quiet your own thoughts, and allow yourself to understand where the other person is coming from. Only then can we have empathy and impactful communication. It starts with listening.

Day 63

Today is not just another day. It is an opportunity, a gift. Is that cheesy? Maybe. But it's also true. It is another moment with friends and family. It is another chance with your colleagues and team.

Today is a day to face your fear, to overcome adversity, to choose to be positive. Today is a day to move forward.

Should you be happy? Why be anything else? Today's air is new. Today's opportunities are new. Today, life is new.

What will you do with it?

Day 64

At what are you great? One of the things that tends to increase our stress level is that we want to be "good" at everything. As a result, we end up being average at many things and great at nothing. We lose our focus and our effectiveness. This translates to our teams as well.

We spread our team thin, not allowing it to fully focus on a specific goal. An average leader has now created an average team.

Simplify your goals, refine your skill set. Focus on becoming great.

Day 65

When things get tough, when you face challenges, when everything seems to be going against you, do you know what you are about? Those few core values that, regardless of the situation, are non-negotiable? The ideals that are at the very center of who you are and the decisions you make?

It's easy — some would say popular — in our world to go whichever way the wind blows. To change your opinion, your direction, your values to fit public opinion. At times, you change based on new information. That is a sign of growth and maturity. To change for convenience, however, is weak.

Know who you are and why you are. In good times and bad, lead from your core values.

Day 66

Are you frozen with fear at the thought of making the next decision? That sounds drastic but leaders are often crippled by pressure. The thought of failing, of making the wrong move or the unpopular decision can cause panic to set in. This can happen in good times and bad.

When things are going well, the pressure intensifies to maintain momentum. When you are in a slump, you feel the tension of needing to turn things around, and quickly.

Don't be controlled by fear. Be confident in you and your team. Confident that your experiences will guide you in the right direction and you can adapt as necessary. The only way to truly fail is to let fear convince you that you should do nothing. Move forward with boldness.

Day 67

Do you celebrate your successes? When you close a deal, complete a project, run a successful campaign, win a title, get a promotion, how do you respond? Do you simply congratulate the team and move on? Aren't the blood, sweat and tears of the people who made the project a success worth more than a simple, "good job"?

Create an environment of celebration. If you quickly move on to the next project, you're creating a team that does nothing more than what is asked. There will be no passion in the work because the people involved aren't being acknowledged for their success. The same goes is true for you. You'll lack excitement and appreciation because you've already moved on.

The next project or challenge isn't going anywhere. Don't be in such a hurry to start it that you fail to celebrate your successes.

Day 68

Are you helping those around grow into the leaders they could be, or are you trying to mold them into the person *you* want them to be? Everybody on your team has the potential to be great - but not necessarily to fit *your* definition of great. Your dreams are not their dreams, your needs are not their passions.

Rather than pressuring people into meeting your vision and needs, equip and empower them to find greatness within their unique identity.

Day 69

When you're dreaming about what could be, planning a new project or campaign, what keeps you from taking the next step? When that voice pops up that causes you to hesitate, what is it saying? As the fear gets louder and louder, to what part of your mind and heart does it speak?

Is it the fear of failure holding you back, or is it the fear of success and the pressure that comes with it? Is it lack of confidence in yourself, or maybe you don't think your team believes in you? Are you afraid of potentially ruining an already good situation? If it ain't broke, don't fix it, right? What if tweaking it takes it to a new level?

Identify the part of your mind where fear speaks loudest to and see it for what it is: a lie. A lie that wants you to embrace safe. A lie that doesn't want you or your team to do great work. Ignore it and get to work.

Day 70

Great leaders are developers. Rather than building a team that mirrors themselves, they develop a team of uniquely skilled individuals. A team that understands its individual and collective strengths and weaknesses. A team that pushes each other to greatness within individual roles, leading to greatness as a team.

Don't let those you lead settle. Always be looking for ways to maximize their skills. Be in the business of developing people.

Day 71

Take a few moments to think of people who are great at something. Not just good or really good, but great. The list is going to be extremely short. We are living in a time where few people truly care about being great.

Homes built today are nowhere near the quality of homes built 100 years ago. It's simply a job to get done, not a craft to perfect. Products are made cheaply so that eventually they break and must be replaced. We chase the comfort of a dollar over the challenge of perfection. We attach our names and legacies to average work.

We shouldn't be OK with that.

Being great isn't easy, of course. It takes years of focused, difficult work. You have to fall in love with your work. You have to dedicate yourself to perfecting your craft. Study, practice, fail, get better, repeat.

If your work is leading people are you going about that lackadaisically, or are you committed to being great?

Day 72

You won the game, had a successful campaign/project, hit your monthly goals. So now what? Those are all terrific and necessary things for success, but where do you go from here? How do you build on it? Complacency destroys growth.

Leadership is about the long term. Focus on creating daily successes that build a sustained movement.

Day 73

What do you think about when you envision yourself, your team, your department, your organization five years down the road? What about 10 years from now?

It's easy to get stuck in our daily routines, unable to see more than five feet in front of us. Our short-sightedness prevents us from dreaming about what could be.

Take time to get away, to look down the road and think about the direction you and your team are headed. Dream about where you want to be and start taking the necessary steps to make that reality.

Day 74

A mission statement is defined as a "statement of the purpose of a company, organization or person, its reason for existing."

Not just words on a page or in a handbook. Not some cheesy statement that sounds good without having any tangible impact on an organization or person.

A statement of *its reason for existing*.

Do you have a personal mission statement? A statement that defines who you are and what you are about. A statement that reminds you of where you are from and where you are going. That provides clarity in the midst of chaos.

If you are lacking direction or often find yourself frustrated, there's a good chance it is because you've never defined your purpose. There's no core to your decision-making, nothing to guide your actions.

A personal mission statement sets a foundation for every decision you make. It brings focus, direction and purpose. It defines your reason for existing. Create one and return to it often.

Day 75

Leadership is often defined as leading or guiding a group of people toward a certain mission. That's an attractive description that people want to sign up for. We all want followers.

How do you get people to follow you? You have to know what they need and how to get them there. How do you know what they need? You have to listen. That's the dirty secret of leadership. It isn't about what you want and need. It isn't about your vision. It's about what your team needs.

Observe what's happening with your team. Listen to their conversations, their dreams. Understand what those people need, then figure out how to get them there.

Day 76

Look back at the last few days and think through where you've spent your time. As you go through today, be intentionally aware of your activities. This goes beyond what is scheduled on your calendar, to examining what you do when you have free moments. Do you head to social media or read an article on your industry? Do you surf the internet or decide to spend time with your team?

We all need time to shut down and take a break for a few minutes, but we must also devote time to growth. It won't happen by chance.

You value what you spend your time on. Do you have time in the day that is devoted to making you and your team better?

Day 77

You can follow the rules. Go by the instruction manual. Stay on the path. Play it safe.

More than likely, that road will lead you to success. Sure, there may be a ceiling to that success but long-term stability sounds great, right?

But will that make you come alive? Will that stir up passion to show up every day? There's something more inside of us. Something that requires our attention, our action.

You weren't made for mediocrity.

Take the risk. Follow your heart. Do work that matters. Watch your leadership come alive as a result.

Day 78

How well do you take criticism? Most of us, if we're honest, don't take it very well. That's natural, of course. We pour our hearts into our work and we want not only to succeed, but to have others appreciate and value our work.

We don't, however, live in a perfect world. Sometimes we screw up and we get criticized. Even when our work is good, it will be at times be criticized. You know what? That's OK.

As a leader, we have to be able to receive criticism of our work for what it is: a unique perspective of our work. It does not mean the person hates us. It doesn't mean they think we're lazy and have bad intentions. They are not taking a shot at us. We have to be able to separate ourselves from our work - which is difficult - and realize that the criticisms are not personal.

Critics are valuable. They show us a new way to view things. They can help us improve, *if* we remove ourselves and listen. Leaders embrace criticism. They don't silence or dismiss it.

Day 79

There's something in us that comes alive when we lean into our fear. It stretches us, causes us to look inside ourselves and find out who we really are. It's easy to act like you believe in yourself when you never take a risk. And acting is exactly what it is.

Once you've faced fear and come out on the other side, then you can really believe in yourself. You realize that the only way to grow, to get better, is to lean in. You learn to embrace fear.

So schedule that meeting you've been avoiding.

Tell the boss about that idea or project you've been thinking about for months but have been too terrified to mention.

Write the blog post you've been too afraid to write, wondering what others in your industry will think.

Apply for that job you've had your eye on but have been too afraid to pursue.

Fear won't get bored and leave. It has nowhere to be. The only way to get past it is to act. Step into it and realize your potential.

Day 80

Everybody has ideas about the way things should be. They can tell you everything wrong about the current situation and why they would have done it differently.

The world is full of problem identifiers.

What's missing is those who do something about it. Those who act. Those who see the problems and, rather than *say* what they would've done, actually *do* something to make it better.

Be more than a critic. Identify problems and fix them. See what could be and find ways to get there. Make things happen.

Day 81

What's the last news story you remember that gave you all of the details? When was the last time you took the time to read through an entire article before commenting on it? On some levels, we are becoming surface people.

Society feeds that through bite-sized tweets/posts and pithy headlines. This impacts our relationships, too. We know the surface level details of our colleagues and friends. We share just enough of ourselves to appease them.

To have depth is to risk. To open yourself up. To ask more meaningful questions of our teams. To go beyond the headline. We have enough surface people. We need people of depth.

Day 82

Would anybody miss you if you stopped coming to work? Would somebody just step in and easily take over your duties, with the department and organization not even missing a beat?

Would they notice if you were gone?

The truth is that most people can do your job (unless, of course, you are a rocket scientist). Nobody, however, can do you.

You should go home every day asking yourself if, regardless of the circumstances of the day, you added value to those around you. It could be your perspective on life, your humor or simply the way you treat people.

Approach each day with the mindset that you are going to make things better. That is a skill that cannot be replaced.

Day 83

Leaders are not about blindly following rules. Strict rules and processes are for managers.

Leaders know when it makes sense to go outside of the rules, to take a left instead of a right. It is not an act of disobedience, but a deep understanding of a situation that goes beyond the rules. Sometimes the right thing to do is to go against the outlined process. When you are dealing with people, you must often throw out the playbook.

Leaders must remember what the end goal is, trust their instincts, and believe in their ability to make it happen. They don't let rules keep them from doing the right thing.

Day 84

Many believe that they will "be a leader" once they achieve a certain status. A status that, typically, is related to job title.

"Once I'm a Manager I'll start leading."

"Once I'm in *that* position, I'll put my ideas to work."

"People will listen to me once I get promoted."

Those are all excuses. Excuses to not speak up now, to not move forward today, to allow things to stay the same. An excuse to take the easy path. And if you're not leading today, why would we trust you to lead tomorrow?

Leadership is not a title or rank; it is a mindset. It is not a position; it is a lifestyle. It does not wait. There is no room for excuses.

Day 85

What if you were bold enough to speak up today?

What if you trusted one of your employees to take the lead on a project while you focused on bigger things?

What if you spoke up about a better way forward for your team or organization?

What if you took a moment to encourage your team members, rather than let their hard work and success go unnoticed?

What if today you said yes instead of your usual no?

What if is the enemy of *what could be.*

Day 86

As much as you try, you cannot control circumstances. A no-lose campaign somehow fails, somebody else gets the promotion or job you want, travel plans are delayed and cancelled, your rock star new hire isn't working out.

Life happens.

What you can control is how you respond. Failure is an opportunity to learn and get better. A missed opportunity allows you to reflect and evaluate. Delayed flights give you necessary time to think through your goals for the week. Bad hires force you to examine interviewing practices and team culture.

Leadership is about a unique perspective. Embrace the opportunity that comes from unexpected moments.

Day 87

Complain or create. You get to choose what you do with each day. You can gripe about traffic, about the weather, about the argument you just had with your spouse, about your boss, about the budget for your department. The list of things you can complain about is endless.

Or, rather than complaining about how you want something to be different, you can create. You can find solutions, make things better, move forward.

Complain about problems or create opportunities. The choice is yours. The only person you need permission from is you.

Day 88

What if you gave your influence away? Your knowledge, experience, your stories, your strengths. The old model of leadership is to hoard all of the information. To be the expert or the guru was to never share your so-called secrets.

Today, everybody has access to the information. What they don't have access to, and what they can't replicate, is you. Give them you.

Day 89

Who says you can't chase your dreams?

Who says you can't go after that big goal, and achieve it?

Who says you can't launch that campaign?

Who says you can't create an amazing culture in your team and organization?

Who says you can't do something that has never been done in your industry?

Who says you can't be a great leader?

The best way to silence the voice that says you can't, is to do.

Day 90

Leadership is influence and influence is power. As a leader, you choose what you do with your power. You can empower people or you can overpower them.

You can use your influence to better others, or you can use it to get what you want. You can serve your team or serve your own interests. The difference between persuasion and manipulation is intent.

How will you use your influence? To empower or overpower?

Day 91

You have the best strategy, you've refined your processes, have a healthy budget, the most talented team and all of the latest and greatest tools that are guaranteed to give your team and organization a direct path to success.

Reality? None of this matters without great leadership. The best teams don't always win. The best strategies are not always executed well. The most money and the best tools guarantee nothing.

The best way to succeed is to invest in your leadership. To understand yourself and your team, and to develop your core that will drive everything you do. Leadership isn't about having the most resources or best plan. It is about consistently developing, inspiring and executing.

Day 92

What am I good at? What am I wired to be? In what environments am I at my best and most productive? These are typical questions leaders (and others) seek answers to. We take tests that identify our strengths so that we can hone in and focus on developing them. We want to operate out of our strengths.

When was the last time we talked about our weaknesses? What will trip me up? What are my stressors?

When you read stories in the news of leaders it is often because they messed up. They were so focused on their strengths that they were blind to their weaknesses.

Know your strengths but don't ignore your weaknesses. We all have our kryptonite. The more we understand what ours is, the more likely we will be to avoid it.

Day 93

We are constantly measuring ourselves. We see how we stack up against others in job title, salary, size of home and kind of car, how new and expensive a suit or outfit looks, how much publicity their team gets - the list is never-ending.

The comparison game is a killer. Especially when you are comparing things that don't really matter.

What's most important at the end of the day is how we influenced people. How we encouraged them, developed them, invested in them, listened to them. It isn't measurable and we can't compare it to the next guy. Maybe there's a lesson in that.

Day 94

Who am I?

What do I want to be known for?

Two questions that we should ask ourselves every day. The answers to those questions should drive the decisions we make, the work we do, the words we use, the way we lead.

Day 95

With every decision you make, you are trying to prove yourself to somebody. It could be your boss, your spouse, your dad, your kids, your team, yourself. It might be more than one person, depending on the situation. You put a significant amount of energy into it. If you're honest with yourself, it might be consuming you.

To whom are you trying to prove yourself to and, more importantly, why? What if you got their approval? The truth is that nothing would change.

You don't have to prove yourself to anybody. Free yourself of that burden.

Day 96

Fear creeps in and whispers, "Why me? Why now?" It tells you that you can't, that you won't, that you shouldn't. Fear hopes to paralyze you.

The world needs you to say to yourself, "Why not me? Why not now? This is my time."

Day 97

True change, true achievement, true leadership doesn't come from being safe. You won't impact anybody sitting behind your desk all day. You won't grow your team and organization by reading books about it. You can't have influence simply by talking about it.

Eventually, you have to get up and do something. You have to take the risk, initiate the conversation, be vulnerable, take the next step. Safe won't get the job done.

Day 98

If you don't start, you won't:

Succeed
Fail
Change
Impact
Learn
Grow
Lead

Take the first step.

Day 99

We fear making a decision because we're afraid of change, but also because we are afraid that, once we've started, we're stuck. There's no turning back.

That's a lie fear wants you to believe.

Change is always an option. There's always a choice to be made, a different direction to go. It may not be easy, it may hurt, but it just might be right.

Day 100

Study great leaders, read about successful organizations, research winning initiatives. Know why they were successful, what made them different.

Don't pressure yourself to mimic them and live up to their standard of greatness or success. They were needed for that specific situation and time.

You are different. You are wired a specific way, have lived a particular life, made unique choices. The sum of those three have brought you to today. Study the greats while operating out of your unique set of strengths. The world doesn't need copycats. The world needs you, at your best.

Day 101

How you view people determines how you treat them. How you treat them impacts your influence. You can't view them correctly if you don't listen to them, ask questions of them, spend time with them. Having more than a surface-level relationship allows you to see them for who they truly are.

You don't have to be best friends with everyone you lead but you must value them. When you value them, you realize they are worth the investment.

Day 102

At the end of the day it's normal to ask yourself, "Was my day successful?" If you ended the day the same place you started, what have you learned? What have you improved? What have you accomplished?

Even if you only moved forward a little bit, it is a success. There is growth in failure. If you learned something from it, you moved forward. An inch is better than nothing. An inch is still forward movement. It is progress.

When asking if your day was successful, what you should be evaluating is if you learned anything, made something better, invested in someone. Ask if you are better at the end of the day than you were at the beginning. Ask if those around you are better than they were when they arrived that morning.

A day is only a failure if you didn't move yourself and those you lead forward.

Day 103

A healthy, motivated, productive team has to do more than simply have belief in the mission or cause. Belief may fuel the fire of now, but eventually those flames will burn out. Impact for the long haul requires a move from belief to commitment.

Committed leaders produce committed teams. Committed teams create real impact. Do you believe in the mission, or are you fully committed?

Day 104

What do you see? When thinking about people, do you first think about their shortcomings? Do you see their failures? When addressing your team, do you talk about what they are doing wrong, why they are missing goals? What about yourself? Is most of your self-talk critical?

What if you looked for the good? In the midst of failure, what if you looked for the successes? What if you looked for what people do well? What if you saw your own wins and positives?

Imagine how our mindset and our interactions (even with ourselves) would change if we looked for positives in every situation.

What we see depends on what we look for.

Day 105

Are you humble? Enter each day and situation knowing that you are in your position to serve others, not to promote yourself. Are you secure? You are a result of your nature, nurture and the choices you've made. Know yourself and your tendencies. What's happened is done and what will happen is up to you. Are you confident? Know what needs to be done, whether that's a new strategy or a specific conversation. Know the role you play in the situation. Prepare and move forward with purpose.

Humble, secure, confident. Three attributes of a leader worth following.

Day 106

During a recent lunch with a friend who is an investor, he asked the question, "How effective is your company?" He followed up with, "Why does your company matter?" He didn't care about how much revenue was generated or what were the margins like. He wanted to know what difference the company is actually making. Money isn't always the driver, and is not always an indicator of success.

Those are two powerful questions not only for organizations, but for us as leaders. "How effective was I today? This week, month, year?" We measure our effectiveness when we define our purpose. What are you trying to accomplish with your life? Not in title or money earned, but at the core of who you are, what are you about?

Leaders don't measure success in dollars. We measure success in the impact we have on the lives of others.

Day 107

The status quo is unacceptable. Settling for mediocrity won't be allowed. What could be won't lose out to what is. Who we were yesterday won't stop us from being who we are meant to be.

Leaders worth following push us forward, leading with the charge of, "Why not us? Why not now?"

Day 108

Your organization is not like the one down the road, or those two you're looking at in your conference. The team you lead is not like the one you invested in at your last job. Your situation is not like the situation you are comparing it to.

Comparison destroys leaders. *You* are what your team needs, today. Lead it how *it* needs to be led, not how you see another team being led.

Day 109

Most leaders are problem solvers. People come to us with a question or concern, seeking direction or help getting unstuck. The natural tendency for us is to dominate that interaction by answering their question and moving on. We have the answer, we have the solution, just listen and do what we say. Problem solved, now on to the next one.

The reality is that this does more harm than good. The only thing others learned from the situation was to come to you for help. Liberating leaders help people come to their own solution. Rather than answering the question, we should respond with a better question (this, of course, requires better listening). We lead them down the path to solving their own problem. This results in them feeling empowered, and owning their solution. They keyword being that it is *their* solution, not *your* solution.

Great leaders don't simply provide answers. They empower by asking better questions to help those they lead arrive at their own solution.

Day 110

Your core values. Your company/organization/team mission. "This is what we're all about." We slap it on our email signature, put it in our employee handbook, insert it into promotional materials, maybe even put it up on the walls. The reality? Values and mission are simply words. Integrity, after all, was a core value of Enron. Words without action are empty.

We don't simply speak our organizational values into being. It's something we as leaders have to commit to living out every day. Values are not an option, they are a demand. A promise. The culture of your team depends on it.

Day 111

Do you love your team? Love is a weird word that probably has some of you feeling uncomfortable and skipping to the next page. I'm not talking about that kind of love. None of that touchy, feely stuff. Do you want the best for those on your team? Are you willing to fight for their best? That's love. To fight for the highest good of another. And to let them know that you're willing to fight for them.

"I'm for you. I see what your best can be and I'll fight for you to get there." When was the last time you said those words? Say them today.

Day 112

Leadership is not a skill to be mastered or a task to be completed. We can't simply check it off our to-do list at the end of the day, week, month or year. We don't wake up one morning as a great leader. There is always something to learn about ourselves and others, always something to improve on.

Becoming a leader worth following is a lifelong pursuit. A commitment to each day becoming better than we were the day before.

Day 113

Too often we treat relationships and interactions as transactional. If you have something to offer me, I'll respect you and listen to you. The truth is that you don't actually respect that person. You're kind to them, but it's only to get what you want. The sale, information, complete the transaction and then leave until you want something else from them.

What happens when you run into someone who seemingly has nothing to offer you? The barista at Starbucks, the receptionist at your dentist's office, the secretary in your own building, your neighbor.

Leaders worth following fight for the highest good of others. *All* others. Everyone has something to offer. Everyone is valuable. Everyone is worthy of respect.

Day 114

In sales, it is common knowledge that you don't make the ask without first developing a relationship. You have to show not only that you have the solution to their problem, but that you are competent and trustworthy.

While we take that approach with potential clients, we rarely put the same effort into developing relationships with our team members. If they don't think we know what we're talking about, we lose influence. If they don't think we're worth working for, we lose influence. Character and credibility create trust. Trust builds influence. Influence opens up the door to leadership. Leadership they want to follow, rather than leadership they have to follow.

Day 115

Most people want to be successful. They want to reach a certain level in their career. They want to get that next promotion. They want to be a good leader. Wanting something isn't enough. The world is full of people who want things. Only the intentional make it happen.

A dream without a plan is just a dream. You won't be the leader you want to be without a plan. Define it, make the plan, then execute.

Day 116

People are watching you. That's creepy, right? But as a leader, you are always being observed. How do you handle stress? How do you handle failure? How do you handle success? Whether you are aware of it or not, those you lead are taking mental notes of your leadership to put to use for the day they are in a leadership position. Your leadership will carry over into theirs - just like you've adopted some of the practices of leaders you've had. What a privilege and huge responsibility that is. This is how your legacy lives on. Not in the day to day tasks you do, but in the style of leadership you model.

What are you showing your team about leadership? Are you modeling what it means to be a leader worth following? Build leaders intentionally, not accidentally.

Day 117

Every day is a battle. You battle people, competitors, budgets, timelines, vendors and more. Battles that take up a lot of our time and our energy. Time and energy that many times is misplaced.

Put more energy into fighting *for* those you lead rather than fighting *against* those on the other side of you.

Day 118

We spend a lot of time trying to fix others. When the team doesn't get the message, when a direct report doesn't respond the way you expected, when there is a sense of constant drama among colleagues. "Why can't *they* listen?" "What can't *they* just do this the right way?" "Why don't *they* listen to me?!"

Unfortunately, the common denominator in most of the drama in our lives is us. If we're not connecting well with others, why? Are we in too big of a hurry? Do we know members of our team well enough to lead them the right way? Are we giving details to those who need details, giving space to dream for those who need to dream? Skills are great, but true leadership comes from being able to connect well with those you lead.

Know yourself to lead yourself. Know your team to lead your team.

Day 119

Leaders are not dictators. They are not order givers, taskmasters, or simply bosses. Leaders help their teams believe that they are working for something bigger. That the work they do each day moves them toward a larger goal. A goal that matters, that changes things.

Leaders remind us that we are here not to simply survive, but to live. In the words of Napoleon, "A leader is a dealer in hope."

Day 120

Is there drama, gossip, unclear communication or lack of commitment among your team? What are you doing about it? If you're allowing it to happen, you're endorsing it. Every time you ignore it, you allow that culture to grow. You're allowing people to believe they are entitled to those actions without being held accountable.

What type of environment are you creating with your words and actions? What about with your inaction? Leaders set culture, either intentionally or accidentally.

Day 121

Our culture tends to listen to and reward the loud. Those who tell great stories and wear their heart on their sleeve draw us in. They naturally connect with us and make us feel welcomed. They breathe life into an organization. The problem happens when we overlook the quiet ones. Those who talk a lot typically do so because that is how they are wired. Extroverts process their thoughts out loud and we become a part of that process. Introverts think before they speak, making sure they have a perfectly crafted, well-thought-out statement. They bring the necessary challenge to the extrovert's big idea. We can't rush through a meeting without giving them an opportunity to talk - typically at the end, so that they've had time to collect their thoughts into a coherent statement.

Leaders worth following recognize that each voice on a team is necessary. They value the quiet thinkers as much as the loud dreamers.

Day 122

When things get difficult do you stick with the plan or do you waver, going with the demands of the crowd? Do you trust in your strategy, knowing you've prepared for the ups and downs, or do you panic and veer off in a new direction? There is a time when we need to adjust our settings, but constantly changing your plan of attack undermines your influence. It shows a lack of credibility and you end up with a team that isn't committed to you or to the work. After all, why work toward this plan when you're going to change your mind in a few months?

When the unexpected happens, the true colors of a leader come out. What will your team see from you in that moment?

Day 123

At swim lessons for my two oldest sons, I noticed a young boy who was terrified of the water. Any time an instructor came near him for his turn, he would start shaking. One instructor kept telling him, "I've got you. I've got you. It'll be OK." The boy wouldn't budge. Finally another instructor came over, put a swim noodle around him, told him to hold tight and lean back. "Lean onto my shoulder. There you go. I'm right here with you." Filled with confidence and more than verbal reassurance, the little guy happily kicked down and back.

We can tell our team all day long what we can do for them and how we can help them. In order to truly lead them, we'll have to show them with our actions.

Leaders don't gain credibility with their words. Credibility comes with actions. Once you've shown you are worth following, your team will gladly follow.

Day 124

What are your feelings toward this week? Are you hopeful, excited, ready? Are you dreading it or completely apathetic? Is today just another day to you, like the one before it and the one after it? Reflect on your mindset, then realize how it impacts the words you'll speak to your team and to those around you. Understand how it determines the actions you take and the decisions you make. Will your team feed off your energy, feeling inspired and ready to attack the day, or will they just complete their tasks and go home?

Your expectations for the day will drive the words and actions of you and your team. What is your mindset? What do you want from today?

Day 125

There's a myth around leadership involving the idea that the leader has to always be "on." Sure, we embrace the role of leader at work, but once we head home for the day, we want to not only leave our work at the office, but also our title/role of leader. The problem with this is assuming that leadership is something you turn on and off. Leadership is not a role or title, it is a mentality. It is a lifestyle. It is a pursuit.

Leaders worth following don't have an on/off switch to their leadership. They realize true leadership is a journey towards being consistent in every area of life.

Day 126

What if you knew how everyone on your team naturally operated? You know that Jeff is good with a deadline but needs space to be creative, while Tiffany needs a detailed project timeline in order to do her best work. You know Jordan loves to speak up and critique ideas (which can sometimes be misinterpreted as critiquing people), while Morris shrinks at the idea of giving feedback in front of the team - but he will open up if you bring him in one on one. You know not only when to support and challenge each person, but how to support and challenge them.

That's an environment everyone wants to be a part of. An environment where people feel known, valued and empowered. That's the kind of team every leader desires to lead. One with clear communication, no drama, and high productivity. The good news is that it's possible for you. Is it hard? Of course. And nobody thinks they have enough time. If not now, when?

To take your team to the next level, you must learn to connect with them. To bring out their best you must know how each operates at their best. Know your team to lead your team.

Day 127

As a parent, you have to be extremely mindful with your actions. Your children hear what you say but, more than anything, they see what you do. My boys are learning from me what it means to be a man, to be a husband, to be a business person, to be a friend. More is caught than taught. How I act impacts how they will act. They repeat my words and they mimic my actions.

The same is true with you as a leader. When you share information with your team, there is a number of ways those people will take and process that information. If it is a task to be done, they will put it through their filter and could end up doing the exact opposite of what you wanted, wasting both their time and yours.

Information transfer doesn't produce change. What matters more from a leader are your actions. You bring your team beside you and say "watch me, imitate me." Every day you show what it means to be a humble, secure, confident leader. Leaders worth following build leaders worth following.

You are your team's example of a leader. You can tell everyone what a leader is or you can show them. Are your actions worth imitating?

Day 128

As a teenager it was my responsibility to mow the yard. I'd start along the outer edge going around the entire yard, then move in one row and do another round, repeating the process until I was done. One time after finishing, and feeling pretty proud of the job I'd done, I went and got my dad. He walked out of the garage, looked at the yard and said, "It would look better if you mowed it diagonally." I was crushed. He wanted the yard mowed, I mowed the yard, but it wasn't enough. I changed my ways and started mowing it diagonally. "Looks good," I thought. Wouldn't you know it, my dad comes out and tells me to go back to the original way. He was always moving the goalposts.

Are you doing this with your team? Right as it really gets going on a project, you change directions. Or maybe when it's finished, you decide to adjust your expectations. The question is why? Did you not clearly communicate your expectations at the beginning or is it that you want to assert your control and power? Either way, you're creating a culture of frustration.

If you're always moving the goalposts on your team, their trust in you erodes. Their work will suffer. Inconsistency undermines influence.

Day 129

Every day we make roughly 35,000 decisions. Decisions that lead to actions - either action by ourselves or by others. For what? What are you moving toward? What are you moving others toward? Is there a purpose that drives your decisions, a why that drives your actions? Or are you just going through the motions, treating each day as if it is independent of the rest of your days?

We don't have time for wasted decisions or words. We don't have time to be lukewarm. I don't want to get to the end of my days and have people say, "He was OK. There's not really much else to say, I guess." I want people to say, "He went for it. He might've been a bit weird but man, he cared about people, he cared about making a difference. Whatever he did, he went all in. Things were better because of him."

If we don't have a why, we're just adding noise to the world. We're taking up space. Leaders worth following pursue a life worth following.

Day 130

Are you the loud dreamer or are you a systems person, preferring to plan every moment of every day? Are you a people person who loves interacting and empathizing with those around you, or are you that guy or girl who needs peace and quiet to gather and process their thoughts? Many of us feel like we're supposed to be something or someone else - especially if we're quiet, as our culture tends to push us toward being the life of the party. We can tend to feel guilty because we don't lead like that other person.

You are wired to be you. You have natural tendencies. While you do need to learn other skills - leadership behavior requires us to use our right and left hand - you can't change who you are.

Will you give yourself permission to be who you are? To lead the way you're wired to lead? You are at your best when you are you, not someone else.

Day 131

From the time we were young, we were trained to chase titles. Be the Student of the Month, the team MVP, the Valedictorian, All-Conference/State/American. That continues as we chase titles and promotions and so-called achievements. The problem with this mindset is that there is never enough. There's always a higher title (or the same title at a larger company), always another board to sit on, always another notch to put in our belt. It causes us to never be satisfied with the now. We end up finding our value in titles rather than in relationships.

Ambition isn't bad, but our value and identity have to come from something else. Something that lasts rather than something temporary.

Titles won't make you happier and they won't make you a better leader. Leaders worth following pursue meaningful connection and impact rather than the next promotion.

Day 132

A kind word can change someone's day. An encouragement or show of support can make her week. You'll be surprised how many people on your team have never had someone tell them that they are for them. To be told they are valued and needed is almost a shock to the system. Many of them are used to leaders using them to get to the next promotion.

Keep showing up. Keep investing in people. Keep showing that they are more than a step on your career ladder. Consistency, credibility and character build influence.

Day 133

Leadership is an ever-changing journey. To get better you must change. You must grow. You must take risks. You must learn new skills and behaviors. You have to open yourself up to your team. You'll screw up, you'll embarrass yourself, you'll create awkward moments. And you'll live through it. Not only will you live through it, you'll learn. Risks lead to learning opportunities. Moments where we can analyze what went wrong, what went right, and why. Moments that helps us better know ourselves and those we lead.

If you are the same leader today as you were a year ago, you're not learning. If you aren't learning, you aren't leading.

Day 134

Last week happened. It had success and failures. Things went as planned and the unexpected happened. Last week was a learning opportunity. Reflect on all that went on. Call out something you can learn from it. Write it down by name. Own your role in it. It's a learning opportunity for you, not someone else. Determine how you can respond to it. What needs to happen for you to get better, to handle the situation differently next time? When will you execute your response? Set a time. Call it. Own it. Response. Execute. A simple, easy way to identify, process and be transformed through a learning opportunity.

Each week is filled with opportunities to learn more about ourselves and those we lead. Intentional leaders look for and respond to them, accidental leaders just move through the days. Keep your eyes open.

Day 135

We've all been in situations where the boss takes time away and everything falls apart. Nobody is sure what to do, everyone is hesitant to make decisions, and nothing gets done. You might be that leader. You try to prove your value by not sharing your wisdom and coaching others. "If they see what happens when I'm gone, they'll know how great I am." Let's call it what it is: self-preservation. To do this is to hold back your team. Rather than building leaders worth following, you're building a team of people who are ill-equipped and afraid. You didn't sign up to be a babysitter, but that's exactly the type of culture you've created.

Start building your bench. Bring people alongside you that you can mentor, to transfer not only your skills but your knowledge. Odds are they want to be in your position someday. That's not a threat, that's an opportunity.

Multiply your leadership. Leaders worth following build leaders worth following.

Day 136

We all have those days where we look up and think, "Really? How is it 6:00?! I didn't get anything done I needed to." Sometimes those days can turn into weeks that turn into months. We get distracted by things that, if we're honest, others can take care of (and if they can't, we're not doing our job as leaders).

What is your main thing right now? The one thing you need to keep in focus? The one thing that plays a role in every decision you make and every task you decide to do. Write it down, keep it in front of you at all times. When distractions pop up, empower your team to act.

When we find ourselves stressed it is typically due to lack of focus. We've spread ourselves too thin and lost sight of what matters. Keep the main thing the main thing.

Day 137

Each person on your team is capable of greatness. If you don't believe that, you've either hired the wrong people or you need to reevaluate your position as a leader. But it's there. Waiting to be seen, waiting to be acknowledged, waiting to be stirred. To fight for the highest good of those you lead is to help them be who they are capable of becoming.

The job of a leader is to see the greatness within those they lead, to get each person to recognize the greatness inside of them, and to make that greatness come to life.

Day 138

When your team sees you coming, do they shrink back in fear or are they happy to see you? When you call them into your office, are they terrified of what's to come or do they look forward to some one on one time with you? When you call a team meeting do they think, "Oh great, what now?" or are they excited to hear what you have to say?

What's it like on the other side of your leadership? Leaders worth following should be a blessing to those they lead, not a burden.

Day 139

After a few years away from the sport, I recently got back into cycling. Though there are some tricks of the trade, so to speak, it isn't a complicated sport. I knew I would be slower than when I had ridden regularly, but I was shocked at just how slow I was and how much I'd forgotten. It felt like I was back in kindergarten learning to ride a bike for the first time - if only I had training wheels this time! Even as I've started to feel more comfortable, there is always something to learn in the sport. From nutrition to technique to equipment to training styles, there is always a way to get better.

Leadership is certainly more difficult than riding a bike. Leadership behaviors are not natural for most of us - if they were, the world would be full of great leaders. We have to use our leadership muscles often to prevent atrophy. You have to be intentional about making time to connect with your team. You have to remind yourself to both challenge and support. To empower rather than overpower. To fight for the highest good of those you lead rather than serve yourself.

If you're not learning and developing every day, your leadership will suffer. You will fall back into your old ways and undermine your influence. You don't one day get a "great leader" plaque to put on your wall. Leadership is a journey, not a destination. Commit to it every day.

Day 140

In a recent conversation with a director of athletics, I asked about the health of his culture. It's a common question to identify areas that are holding back the organization, areas that may be blind spots to some. His response was quite typical. "Well, we don't all sit around, holding hands and singing Kumbaya, if that's what you mean."

There's this idea among many leaders that a "healthy" culture is one where everyone is best friends and gets along without argument. I would argue that an environment like that is anything but healthy. You've created a culture of protection, where everyone is afraid to speak the truth, to call out the real problems that they see. This leads to entitlement ("they've never held me accountable, so they can't start now") and mistrust.

Teams with a healthy culture disagree, sometimes passionately. After all, you're talking about different people with different personalities. The key is in how they disagree. Healthy teams speak the truth without making personal attacks, and those on the receiving end trust the opinions of those bringing the challenge. It's about calibrating both support and challenge.

A team without disagreement is a team that won't last. Healthy teams understand how to disagree well, knowing that each person is fighting for the highest good of the team.

Day 141

I'm convinced that most of the greatest ideas in the world (past and present) never leave the heads of those who come up with them. Fear creeps and tells them that they aren't good enough, that nobody will ever listen, that the risk is too great. Who knows what world-changing ideas have been left on the cutting room floor of our minds? That's not a battle fear should win.

What ideas do you need to bring to your team today? What words do they need to hear, what story do you need to invite them to join? Maybe even more critically, have you created an environment where those you lead are scared to share their big ideas?

Be bold enough to bring life to your thoughts and dreams. They do no good if they never leave your head.

Day 142

One thing a leader cannot do too much of is communicate. Those on your team don't know what you are thinking or what you want if you don't tell them. You shared your grand vision but you didn't tell them exactly what you want. Never assume that they know what you expect. When you assume and fail to communicate, you set everyone up for disappointment and bitterness. You are bitter towards them because they didn't live up to your unspoken expectations, and they are bitter towards you because you are impossible to please.

Leaders worth following bring clarity. They take the time to communicate, and communicate again.

Day 143

"I want to be a leader worth following." That's a statement you've made or at the very least, a statement you believe. If you want it, if we want it, we'll have to fight for it. It isn't easy. You'll have to sacrifice. You'll have to commit to people even when they disappoint you. You'll have to push against the status quo, against the years of poor leadership those on your team have endured (from others and, maybe, from you). You'll have to fight alongside those you lead when they struggle, when they want to give up, when they don't feel like they are good enough.

You'll have to fight your own mind, the demons that constantly show up telling you that you can't lead people, that they'll never follow you. You'll have to understand how you're wired, why you think and act the way you think and act.

You'll take risks because the relationships are worth it. You'll do the hard work of knowing, truly knowing, your team. When do they need space? When do they need direction? You'll support when people need to be supported and challenge when they need to be challenged.

People will wonder what in the world you're doing. They'll wonder why you don't take the easy way out. Why you don't fire that difficult person instead of believing in and apprenticing them. They'll question why, instead of taking the job at that bigger, better program, you choose to believe in the power and potential of where you are.

And then they'll see your team. They'll see how you operate. How you communicate. How everyone is on the same page, moving the same direction. They'll see how you debate and how you celebrate. They'll see that you've actually built a team of leaders worth following. They'll think, "I'm not sure what's going on, but our team needs that. I need that."

Know your team, fight for your team, lead your team with a passion that others think is just crazy. I can't think of anyone who wouldn't want to follow a leader like that.

Day 144

Ego (insecurity masked as pride) causes us to do things we wouldn't normally do. It makes us think we're more important than the people around us. It makes us think we deserve more than they do. It makes us think we're entitled to something. It makes us think our role is more important than their role. It causes us to shave a little off the top (after all, we've earned it), to do a little less (once you get to a certain point, aren't you above some of the work?), to create our own rules.

Ego must go. It is a threat to your culture and, if ignored, will destroy it. Every person matters, every role matters, nobody is better or deserves more or is entitled to anything but being respected and valued.

Day 145

Checking your phone during a meeting with a friend, co-worker or direct report. Finishing up that email while your 9:00 is sitting in your office waiting to talk with you. Walking into your house while on the phone, rather than with both hands free and ready to greet your family. Talking more about your ideas rather than listening to others. Forcing your business talk into a comfortable, social setting.

Simple things we do every day that hinder our ability to connect with those we lead. Things that undermine our influence. If we disconnect, we hurt our ability to lead. People matter enough to get your undivided attention.

Day 146

As a leader, you cannot be lukewarm. You are either all in or fully out. If you are not all in, you'll lack the passion and commitment needed to encourage and lead your team through this project or season. That lack of enthusiasm will be see as doubt and apathy, which will kill morale, creativity and production.

Your teams needs to feel your genuine passion. Your teammates need to know it means something to you. They need to know you believe in the work they are doing. Show up with purpose and dedication.

Day 147

Pay attention to how you speak to your team. Not just what you say but the tone and tact.

Pay attention to how you act around your team. By what you are saying with those actions. By what you are saying and showing is acceptable.

Pay attention to your attitude in conversations, in meetings, while you're working.

Without thinking about it, our words, actions and attitudes have significant impact on our team. That impact can be good or bad. We are showing the team what we value. And those are all things we can control.

Culture isn't just what you say, it's what you do and how you do it.

What if your team spoke to each other the way you did, acted the way you did, had your attitude? Is that a team you'd want to be a part of? Leaders set the tone.

Day 148

If we want food, we can have almost anything we want within minutes. If we want to watch a TV show, we have it at the push of a button. If we need the oil changed in our car, we can have it done within the hour. We have everything we need at almost any time we want.

The problem is we expect the same for our teams. The team isn't communicating well and I want it solved today. The team doesn't trust each other and I need that changed before the end of this meeting. Our revenues aren't where we want them to be and I want it fixed this month. My players aren't engaged and I need it fixed at practice.

We're an impatient people. Much like Veruca Salt in *Willy Wonka and the Chocolate Factory*, we want it all and we want it now. But culture doesn't work that way. It takes conversations and vulnerability and repaired relationships and intentional communication and to start it all over again the next day and the next and the next. It takes time and it takes patience.

No matter what any book says or any speaker says or any inspirational quote says, there is no quick fix for culture. There is no quick fix to becoming a great leader.

We live in an instant gratification world but there's nothing instant about building great culture. Dig in and do the work.

Day 149

How do people feel when they walk into the office? Are they excited about the work they're about to do? Are they defeated, believing that their effort doesn't matter? Are they frustrated and bitter, believing they deserve something better?

What about when you walk into a room? Do people stop talking and fearfully look down to begin working, or are they happy to have you around?

Culture is the atmosphere your team is breathing in and out every day. It is either giving them life or draining their energy. Leaders define culture.

Day 150

When things go wrong, who gets the blame? Competitors? Your team? The industry? Bad timing? Often, we are the last person we place blame on. It makes sense, of course. If we aren't responsible, we can't be held accountable. We can always point our finger somewhere else.

This is the mark of an insecure leader. It's a role I played for far too long (and a role I fight against every day).

When we own the issues, our influence rises. "That's on me. I made the wrong choice and it hurt our team. I'm sorry." When is the last time you heard a leader say that? How much respect would you have for one that did?

Only when we own our role can we get better.

Insecure leaders shun accountability so they can avoid responsibility. Secure leaders know that being accountable helps them grow and succeed.

Day 151

Patience is something few of us have. We want to get started, to run forward, to figure out the details along the way. "We've talked about it enough, let's get going. If you ain't first, you're last."

For some, like me, that strategy is just fine. For those who need details and need to have a few steps outlined and reassurances made before they fully commit, this strategy creates frustration and mistrust. What we tell these people is that we don't have time for their questions, which makes them feel like we don't have time for or value them.

And when we run forward without taking the time to process the plan, we get a team of people running at different directions and different speeds. Teams can thrive when everyone is running in the same direction at the same pace. And slowing down to answer what can feel like frustrating process questions might actually bring clarity to a better path forward, that saves even more time (and money). Velocity = speed + alignment.

Great leaders take the time to make sure the team is all on the same page before moving forward. Every voice matters and has value. Slow down to speed up.

Day 152

An observation I've made after spending a lot of time with leaders, is that many of them (and at times I am certainly included in this group) want to be a great leader, and they talk the talk of a great leader, yet they don't live their words.

Many of us preach positivity while being negative. Many of us preach collaboration while isolating ourselves. Many of us preach clear, consistent communication while always changing our message and direction.

This lack of authenticity undermines our influence and destroys our teams. Our team simply tunes us out, knowing that tomorrow's message will be different. The good news is that there is an easy solution. Simply do what you say.

You can't lead what you don't live. Authentic, consistent leaders build trust and lead connected, championship teams.

Day 153

Hope is absurd. It is irrational. It is a threat to the status quo. Hope drives our dreams and gives us energy to pursue what others think is not only impossible, but crazy. Hope sees what people and teams and industries are capable of being. Hope sees how ideas can change one heart, which is all we need to change the world.

Hope is contagious and it refuses to allow us to settle.

Hope is not a strategy, but it is a characteristic of a leader worth following. Let a hope for what could be drive you to pursue and create what will be.

Day 154

You preach at your team. You teach your team. Throwing out bits of information here and there, bits of strategy here and there. "If only they knew what to do. If only they knew what I know." While information can certainly be a barrier for success (especially if we're talking about new employees or players), it typically isn't the main cause. The main cause is a lack of knowing why.

Your players need to know things you know, but they also need to know why. They need to know how this information has played out in your life and what it means for them. This leads to them not only knowing what to do, but also why to do it (or not to do it).

The same is true in our leadership development sessions. We can tell leaders they need to connect, we can tell them they need to balance presence and productivity, we can tell them they need to communicate in a different way. The reality is that this is stuff most of them know already. But they've not been told why. They've not been given a real reason to do things differently. They've not been shown what it's like to be on the other side of their leadership. Information doesn't change that. Transformation does. Once that information becomes relevant to them, once it becomes practical and applicable, then they start to choose new actions.

The "what" informs teams, the "why" makes them come alive.

Leadership is sharing what you know and why it matters. It leads to transformation, not just a transfer of information. Lead intentionally.

Day 155

Dealing with people is frustrating, isn't it? They never seem to do exactly what we want, or be exactly who we want them to be. Regardless of your position, this is true. (side note: when you do get to be in a position of leadership by title, remember that you were once on the other side. Remember what it felt like and the resistance you put up.)

We critique and we direct and we hope people change. The reality is that we can't make people change. No matter how hard we try no matter how much we invest, ultimately it is up to them. They have to decide they want to be better. They have to decide they're capable of more.

What leaders do is help people see that. Paint a picture of what could be and provide daily support and challenge to put them in a position to take advantage of it. Remind them of that daily. The rest is up to them. Go up the mountain before them and show them it's possible, then guide them along their own path up. You are their sherpa.

The job of a leader is not to change people. The job of a leader is to help people see who and what they're capable of being, and empower them to be it.

Day 156

Leadership isn't completing tasks and running meetings and giving orders. It's taking the time to teach others, to invest in others, to empower others.

Leadership does not mean you've solved everything, that nobody can speak truth into your life, that you've learned all there is to learn. It's having the humility and self-awareness to know that you can always get better, that there is always someone to learn from, that you should always have someone you are accountable to, someone who can tell you, "No."

Two questions to reflect on at the end of each day:

Who got better because of me?

Whom did I allow to make me better?

Day 157

In a recent coaching meeting, we were discussing a member of this individual's leadership team with whom they were having a difficult time. This person had spent the better portion of a year too prideful to accept help and constantly trying to prove that he belonged in his position. As a result, he had alienated the people he was leading, alienated the leadership team and turned the board against him. Those who were advocates and tried to offer genuine help along the way, have now given up and essentially said, "You're on your own."

How often do we do the same thing? In an attempt to prove our worth or our intellect or our skills, we end up doing just the opposite. We burn ourselves out, undermine our influence, and eventually look around to find that we're on our hill alone.

People are drawn to leaders with humility, to leaders who accept help, to leaders who admit they don't know it all and can't do it all.

The constant need to prove yourself will ultimately end up pushing others away. Leaders worth following are secure, confident and humble.

Day 158

Look in the headlines each day and you see examples of companies that value the wrong thing. How do we know what they value? Look at their actions. When you value money more than other things, you make decisions based on how much money you can make. When you value policies and procedures, you make decisions based on rules (rules are good but there are times when doing the "right" thing is in fact going against what your policies say). When you value status, you make decisions based on what keeps you feeling powerful.

You can say you value you something but your actions show what you really value. Your team passes that on to those they lead and serve (players, fans, customers, recruits, donors, alumni).

When you value people, your actions show it. You make decisions that reflect that value. Your team hears and sees it, and those values get passed on. It creates and multiplies a culture that fights for the highest good of those you lead.

What do you value? Don't look at your mission statement. Look at your actions. Whom and what do they benefit? It may not be what you think and it may not be what you say.

Your culture is a reflection of your values, and your values guide your actions. Leaders must speak and live the values. Leaders define culture.

Day 159

There are demands on your time, pulling you away from your people and convincing you that you don't have time to invest in them. Notifications and meetings and a number of other distractions keep you and your team from connecting. Pride, ego and fighting for your own interests builds a gap in the trust your team has in each other. Deadlines and budgets and family issues and recruiting classes and donor meetings are adding stress to each day as the pressure to produce and win builds.

There is a battle against your culture and each day it starts over. You can show up accidentally each day, simply completing what's on your calendar for the day, or you can show up and make your culture a priority. You control the decisions you make, you control how you communicate, you control what you value, you control whether or not you invest in your people. Leaders define culture — every single day.

Time, distractions, ego and stress are working against your culture. If you don't show up on purpose, they win. Fight for your culture daily.

Day 160

As leaders, we're under a crazy amount of pressure. Everyone around us wants results. And now. They want more wins, more money, more buildings, more highly ranked recruits, more revenue, more profit, more sales, more followers, more, more, more. Tomorrow is too late.

This pressure creates stress. And none of us - I don't care who you are - operate well under extreme stress. Our default is to get angrier, to demand more, to cut corners, to run and hide, to overwork. We feel that pressure every day, but we have a choice in how we respond.

Stress, unfortunately, causes many of us to take shortcuts. We turn a blind eye to issues, convincing ourselves we can make it work. We twist the truth with that donor or that co-worker, justifying it internally because we didn't really lie, did we?

These actions that get us a "win" today are compromising our culture in the long run. They are tiny actions that seem minor in the moment, yet as they build up, they become significant cracks in our foundation.

The flip side is that we can communicate clear, realistic expectations. We can be honest with what we expect and what our team can expect from us. We can acknowledge the reality of where we are today, with a hopeful vision and plan for what will be. Your situation didn't get to where it is overnight and a championship culture won't be built overnight. It will take time, but you'll have a foundation that will last over time and produce better results than anyone could have imagined.

An obsession with winning immediately will cause you to cut corners. Focus on building a culture that will produce a legacy of success.

Day 161

If you're frustrated with your people and your culture, look in the mirror. We set the tone. If we're for ourselves, we'll create individualistic teams. If we're lazy, we'll create teams that don't produce. If we're pessimistic, we'll create teams without belief.

If you want a better team, be a better leader. Don't hope people grow; help them get to the next level. Don't hope they communicate better; create a culture where communication is clear and consistent. Don't hope they take ownership of the work; create a culture where all know their roles and do their part to fight for the good of the person next to them.

Great leaders create great culture that attracts great talent - then they develop that talent. Changing culture starts with you.

Day 162

You lose a game, a large donor stops giving, a staff member leaves, a player gets hurt, two competitors merge, the industry is struggling, budget cuts are coming.

Your team goes one of two ways. People start blaming each other, griping about how "so and so" screwed this up "like they always do." Gossip builds and trust erodes. After a while, things settle down, but the pain and scars are still there as the issues went unaddressed.

Or they look at each other, see what they've done and see the next steps, see who needs to be picked up, see who needs an encouraging word and who needs to be challenged, and they step up.

Culture isn't made in these moments; it is revealed.

Under pressure, unhealthy teams point fingers and fight each other. Healthy teams take ownership of their roles and fight for each other.

Day 163

Tomorrow you'll have the conversation you've been putting off.

Tomorrow you'll share that vision that would change the trajectory of the team.

Tomorrow you'll encourage that co-worker who has been struggling.

Tomorrow you'll empower those around you to be their best.

Tomorrow, tomorrow, tomorrow.

Tomorrow is the enemy of culture. You'll always be waiting for the "right" time to start. Stop making excuses; start doing the work.

Day 164

Maybe you walked in to the office today and were frustrated by the lack of communication on your team.

Maybe you're tired of the drama. Of the confusion. Of the lack of vision. Of the fact that people are driven by ego and not by the love of their teammates.

What will you do about it? You can point fingers and demand people get better, but when has that ever worked? Or you can ask what is going on, find out what is at the root of the problems, and call people up to a better way of life and leadership. You can go first. You can be the standard.

If your culture isn't what you want it to be you have two options: complain about it or change it. Leaders take action. Do the hard work.

Day 165

When you don't value the voices of those you lead, they stop speaking up. You lose the practical wisdom of those who bring logical clarity. You lose the relational depth of those who intuitively know how each person will react to a new idea. You lose the outside the box thinking of the dreamers. You lose the collaborative impact of those who cheer on the team to greatness.

When your voice and vision are all that matter, every other voice becomes one of quiet, defeated agreement. They suppress their gifts that bring life and energy to the team, and simply fall in line. We don't see it right away, but this becomes reality over time. The work becomes something to complete that day, rather than something with purpose.

When people don't feel valued or understood, they don't bring their best to the team. They stop speaking up, which causes leaders to operate without the full truth of what's going on and become someone the team *has* to follow.

When people are heard and appreciated, they come to life and thrive. They bring energy and purpose each day, even during difficult seasons. Leaders who create this environment are leaders that people choose to follow.

Winning teams harness the gifts of their people, utilize their expertise and empower every voice to bring their best to move forward.

Day 166

Do you believe in the people you call your team? Do you think, regardless of their current level of performance, that they're capable of greatness? That they are capable of being leaders?

Does your conversation about them reflect that, or do you complain about them at every turn? What about the words you speak *to* them - are they encouraging and supportive and empowering, or are they belittling and critical?

Words matter. People become the conversations we have about them, and the words we speak over them. Be intentional in calling your team up to the greatness that is inside of it.

Day 167

"Is she for me, against me, or for herself?"

With every interaction and every decision, your team is asking themselves that. What you say matters, but what you do must match. If you say you want them to win, do your decisions reflect that? If you say you value their voices, are you giving them a chance to be heard?

It's about intent and it impacts trust. When making a decision and before engaging in conversation, check your intent. Are you doing what's best for you, what will hurt your team (this is rare, but it happens), or what's best for the team?

When you're for them, they trust you. Your actions set the tone for a selfless team that fights for the highest good of one another. When you're not, those same people lose trust and they focus on what's best for them. Your actions have given them permission to be selfish. To fight for their own highest good, no matter what it costs the team.

A championship culture is built on trust. Without it, your team turns inward. Trust builds connection which builds commitment. Be worth following.

Day 168

Stress happens to every leader and every team. I went two years with no paycheck while trying to build Fieldhouse Media (and another failed business). No matter how great your culture is, life happens. There are certain stresses a great culture can avoid (drama, miscommunication, etc) but there are things that are beyond your control.

You can't control what comes at you but you can control how you respond. When fear and doubt and negativity come in, you can choose to kick them out. Attitude is a choice. If I had given up (and believe me, the voices of doubt and fear and negativity weren't just whispering, they were screaming), I wouldn't be in the position I'm in today. Nothing is easy but if you believe the vision, you choose to be positive and you keep going.

If you go negative, your team goes negative. And it's a hard place to escape. If you believe, and you fight for your team, those folks will believe. They'll fight together and for each other. It doesn't mean it will be easy, but it will be possible.

Positive leadership isn't about ignoring a negative reality. It's about not being defined by it and choosing a hopeful way forward.

Day 169

In the midst of erratic days where any moment can be thrown off by a meeting, a phone call or anything else we deem "urgent" in the moment, what in our days is consistent? What looks the same, no matter the time or place?

If the answer is nothing, we have a culture of chaos and confusion. It is a broken culture where everyone is moving in his own direction. This is one of the reasons we spend a lot of time working with programs to build a common language. It creates clarity, eliminates confusion and allows people to move forward together.

What kind of culture do you want? What behaviors will make that a reality? What is stopping you from doing those today?

Culture is created through consistent behavior. Define and communicate it, then celebrate the behaviors that bring it to life. Lead intentionally.

Day 170

"Winning solves everything" is a common saying in the sports world - and I've heard it in many businesses as well. From team drama to lack of donor support to poor engagement on social media, many simply believe that winning is the obvious fix.

While a healthy culture will lead to winning, winning is not always a reflection of healthy culture. Sometimes winning actually masks the issues that are going on. You're frustrated with this teammate, but you're winning so you don't say anything. One of your best players is being selfish and distancing himself from the team, but you're winning, so you let it slide.

Once you have a few losses or setbacks, those things you let slide will suddenly become red alerts. They're a crisis waiting to happen, simply because you ignored them while things were "good" since the team was winning.

Great leaders balance support and challenge in good times and bad. They know that culture is a journey, not a destination. The work is never done.

Winning doesn't solve everything and doesn't mean you have a healthy culture. You have to battle for your culture daily. Lead intentionally.

Day 171

A compelling vision will engage your people — temporarily. Incredible facilities and benefits will impress your people — for a while. A new title or a little more money or some recognition will get their attention — for the moment.

These things are all temporary fixes. They're good and you should do them, but it treats your people as something less than they are. They are humans. They have stories. They have hopes and dreams and fears and failures and successes. They have families and they have lives.

To get and keep their attention, to get them engaged, to get them committed, you have to know and connect with them as people. Over lunch, over filling up your coffee in the break room, while walking to a meeting or heading out on a road trip, talk to them. Really talk to them. Ask them questions and find out who they are and why they are. When people feel known and valued, they show up with passion and purpose.

You have a choice in how you treat your people. You can trot out shiny new objects to get their attention, or you can give them your attention.

If you want an engaged team, get to know them as people. When you know them, you can connect with them. When you connect, they'll commit.

Day 172

One of a leader's main responsibilities is to bring clarity. Clarity about the present and about the future. Clarity around roles and expectations. When there is clarity, there is purpose. When there is purpose, teams can be connected. When they are connected and clear on the purpose, they are focused. The sky is the limit.

When there is a lack of clarity, they get confused. They are confused about what's going on and where they're going. They're confused about who is doing what and why. They don't know what is being measured. When they are confused, they disconnect. They start focusing on themselves and their personal agendas. They get distracted by what's going on outside the team. They chase paths that take them away from the goal.

A lack of clarity that leads to a disconnected and disengaged culture will take out even the most talented team.

A disconnected team will easily be distracted by outside noise and criticism. A connected team stays focused on the vision and each other.

Day 173

When you're wrong, you don't need to hide it. You don't need to spin it. You don't need to try to justify it. You don't need to lie about it. You don't need to ignore it.

You'll be wrong dozens of times today. That's OK. Nobody is perfect and your team certainly doesn't expect you to be. Being wrong isn't a weakness and admitting you are wrong certainly isn't a weakness. We convince ourselves of that, but it's a lie we must choose not to believe.

When you ignore and hide and lie about your mistakes, you undermine your influence. You lose the trust of your team, which results in losing the commitment of your team. You also create a culture where others can do the same. They can lie and hide and justify their mistakes. Leaders set the tone.

What happens when you admit your mistakes is that your influence grows (unless you're constantly apologizing for the same mistake - that's just laziness). Your team trusts in your integrity and humility. People feel they can bring their issues to the table as well. And when we bring mistakes to the light, we can start to fix them. The team improves and is more connected.

Admitting you're wrong is a strength, not a weakness. Leaders who own their mistakes create a culture of humility and accountability.

Day 174

When I'm insecure, I do what's best for me. I get defensive and prideful and I let my ego lead me. When I find my identity in my job, I feel like I always have something to prove and something to lose. As with insecurity, it causes me to focus on me. I lose sight of what's best for the team and for my family. I focus on my wants, my needs, my ego. I let things slide that I would typically deem unacceptable. I justify it because winning solves everything. If it gets me closer to my goal, it has to be good, right?

Most leaders are the same way. We start out with the right intentions but as we gain influence and power, self-preservation and insecurity set in. We think someone is always after our position and/or that someone is always doubting us.

This kind of leadership is constricting for a leader and their teams. You create pressure and as you feel it closing in, you reflect it onto your team. Instead of focusing on the vision, everyone focuses on which direction we're going to go today and how to can keep up.

It's a vicious cycle, but we can stop it. We can choose to be secure, confident and humble. We can choose to be for our team. We can choose to kick our ego to the side. But it's an every day choice.

Insecurity and self-preservation cause good leaders to make bad decisions. Keep your focus on your team. Lead with humility, not ego.

Day 175

For many leaders, culture is all talk. They have the phrases down and the slogans memorized and they drive into their team the importance of culture. Then they turn around and do the opposite. They do what's best for them, not what's best for the team. They act for the good of themselves, so their teams do the same. Leaders define culture not just with their words, but with their actions.

A recent study I read suggested that less than 10% of organizations create winning culture. For all of the talk about culture in our world, less than 10% are acting on it. This could be because they don't know what to do, but also because they don't want to do the hard work. They want to speak culture into being, not work it into being.

Building culture is fun to talk about but hard to do. It takes commitment, it takes perseverance, it takes being willing to admit when you mess up and say what you're going to do to get better. Creating a championship culture is counter-cultural. Otherwise everyone would do it. If you're willing to put in the work, your team will follow and the results will come.

Talking about culture is not the same as creating culture. Great leaders turn that talk into action, and empower their teams to do the same. Leaders set the tone.

Day 176

"We have big issues." "Our team is never on the same page." "I feel like I'm speaking German." "We have talent but we're not a team."

A majority of the teams we work with are in the midst of or on the edge of crisis. They are hitting extreme stress and they're feeling the pressure of their culture caving.

There's never a bad time to invest in your culture but what would it look like for you to do it today? To be proactive instead of reactive? To acknowledge that things might be OK today, but that your culture must be built to last.

Stress will hit every team. Your culture will determine whether you cave or persevere, and how. Don't hope for culture, create it. Today.

Day 177

Leadership can often seem like it's for "them" and not us. It's for the top 10%, not the other 90%. It's for those with titles who sit in offices, not us in the cubicles or at the end of the locker room.

When we believe that, we're giving ourselves an out. We're abdicating our opportunity and responsibility. We're wasting what influence we have. We're saying, "Since I'm not one of them, I don't have to lead. I don't have to own the situation. I don't have to step up. I don't have to speak up."

Leadership is a muscle. Everyone has it, we just have to develop it. We have to practice, we have to work at it. It will be easier for some than it is for others, but anyone can become a great leader. Anything great will require hard work and will be worth it.

Insecure leaders believe that leadership is for the few and they use that to keep control and power. Secure leaders know that a team of leaders is better than a team of "yes" men.

Leadership is for you, it's for everyone. It's a skill that requires practice and work. The more you do it, the better you become. Show up today. Nobody is stopping you.

Day 178

I recently walked a team through one of our culture building programs. When I walked in, I noticed several words on the office and locker room walls. *Family. Together. Positive. Committed.* I remembered seeing the same words in the email signature of my contact there.

As we walked through the reality of their culture, different words came up. *Disconnected.   Frustrated.   Lack   of   Communication. Individualism.* Stuff was getting done, but the culture was fractured. They were operating at 54% health (based on our internal survey).

Many leaders we encounter think that simply by giving a speech and repeating certain phrases or values, that the team will magically embody those traits. They often fail to look in the mirror and realize that they are not living those values themselves, and that the team is simply following their lead.

Culture is not a mission statement (though that's part of it). Culture is not a list of stated values (though that's part of it). Culture is not a speech (though that can be part of it). You can do all of those things, and still have a place where people dread showing up. Our words must be followed by consistent actions. Leaders set the tone.

And if you're not the leader in terms of title, no excuses. You determine your personal culture. You can still show up with positivity. You can still choose to communicate clearly. You can choose to be for the person next to you. You can raise the bar, and call those around you up to that level - not with pride, but with humility. Not because you're better, but because they're all capable of it.

Culture is how your team feels when their alarm clock goes off in the morning. Create an environment where people are excited to take part.

Day 179

I'm not the same leader I was a year ago. I communicate differently. I challenge differently. Why? Because I expect a different team, a different family, a different life if I'm the same. I screw up every day, multiple times per day, but I can't settle for sameness.

The same is true of you with your team. Are you a better leader than you were a year ago? If not, why? And what impact is that having on your team? If we want our team to be better, we have to start with ourselves. We have to show the willingness to work and grow, and the transparency to admit we have room to grow. We have to be the culture we want. Not just our words, but our actions.

You can't hope for change without changing. Your culture won't get better unless you do. It's hard and awkward but worth it. Leaders go first.

Day 180

You go into each day wanting to do what's best for you. Throughout the day you are constantly frustrated when people on your team make decisions that are clearly not best for the team, but benefit only themselves.

You change direction each day, in order to pursue goals that fit your ambitions. Then you get frustrated when people on your team undermine your decisions by doing what get's them closer to their personal goals.

You do what's convenient for you each day, then can't understand why your team doesn't buy in. People ignore the vision you laid out and do what's easiest for them.

In working with a team recently, one we've been working with for several months, I noticed a significant shift in mindset, communication, engagement and productivity. I asked the team (not the leader) what happened.

The consistent answer? "He's thinking about us now, instead of thinking about himself." It causes the team to commit, even when times are difficult. It causes teammates to work together, because their leader is modeling that behavior. It causes them to care, because they feel heard and cared for.

When they felt ignored and used, it was easy to ignore the leader and look out only for themselves. When they felt valued, that kind of behavior was not only unacceptable, it wasn't even considered.

If you're for yourself, your team members will be for themselves. If you're for the good of the team, they will be as well. Leaders define culture.

Day 181

We want our team to be great, yet we're afraid to do what it takes to create a culture that allows for greatness. We want our team members to communicate well, yet we're afraid to show them we value their opinion. We want to be the leader we're capable of being yet we're afraid to screw up, to risk our reputations, to be uncomfortable.

Over and over again in our conversations with leaders, there is a desire for what could be that is overtaken by fear.

Fear is a lie. Fear shows up where it is allowed to stay. Fear is what keeps good leaders from being great, and keeps good teams from being championship teams.

Fear forces you to settle for what is rather than fight for what could be. We won't reach our capabilities unless we take the next step.

Day 182

Your team members are not there for you to use for your own good. They are not pieces on your chessboard to be moved around to your advantage. They are not line items on a budget. They are not titles on an organizational chart or roster.

They are humans. Humans with wants and needs and desires and dreams and skills and ideas.

Though most of us agree with this, we don't always lead as though we believe it. In the midst of our task-driven, me-focused world, we tend to think everything is about us and our wants and our careers. Slowly, accidentally, we become for ourselves and undermine our influence.

The good news is that how we see people and how we lead people is our choice. We can choose to value them as people, we can choose to believe they matter, we can choose to believe that they are capable of greatness. We can choose to be about more than our own wants.

If you see your team as employees/players, you just want them to produce. If you value them as people, you'll fight for their highest good.

Day 183

Maybe you're frustrated with the lack of production from those on your team. Maybe it's the lack of communication, or how focused on themselves they tend to be. Little things are becoming big things. Small frustrations are turning into large divides.

This may be too simple, but have you said anything? Or are you sitting by, complaining in your head without actually speaking up or doing anything about it? Are you letting the little things slide, are you not communicating well, are you focused on yourself?

Teams have issues. After all, we're people and we're far from perfect. Many times when we're working with teams, it's become the norm for nobody to speak up. Everyone one is frustrated, everyone expects better, but everyone keeps that inside. Uncommunicated expectations are premeditated bitterness. Lay out the expectations, communicate them clearly, then do what needs to be done to help your team meet them.

Your teammates can be great. They can communicate, they can produce, they can have humility and be connected. That kind of culture starts with you (regardless of your position/title).

Is your team mediocre because your culture allows it to settle? Call people up into who they are capable of being. Leaders set the tone.

Day 184

We can spend all day focusing on the work. What must be done and how? Who will do this project and who will prepare this document and will it be ready on time? Make sure this analysis is ready for this meeting and make sure he knows where to be and when.

Tasks, emails, meetings, projects, practice.

Where is there time for the vision? Where is there time to remind where we're going and why? The work is being done, but do the team members care about it, or are they just checking it off of their lists? Is it being done with purpose or passion?

A team without heart is a team without impact. The what and the how matter, but leaders must constantly be reminding the team of the why.

Day 185

Many of us are desperate for the attention and validation and praise from others. If only that person would acknowledge us, we would feel like we're good enough. If only she would pay attention to us, she'd see how great we are. If only he would tell us and others how good we are, we would feel complete. Yet when our focus is on the opinions and validations and praise of others, we neglect our team.

The noise - good or bad - from the outside doesn't matter. We aren't who others say we are, we are who our team says we are. Our focus should be on it.

You'll become a better leader when you stop worrying about attention and praise from others, and start giving attention and praise to your team.

Day 186

A leader I worked with recently noted his frustration with his team for not speaking up. "I feel like I'm constantly having to pull them along." As we broke it down (trying to focus on what his role in the problem has been, rather than focusing on what's wrong with the team), he realized he's been disconnected and a taskmaster. He's focused on what they're doing wrong rather than actually connecting with them to understand why things are going wrong. They don't have an opportunity to speak up, and whenever they do, they get bit, so they keep quiet.

Sound familiar? This is a situation we run into with team after team. And to fix it, we have to look within. We have to focus on the people, not the process, the team and not just the work. If we want them to speak up, we have to provide that opportunity.

A leader who doesn't listen will have a team that doesn't speak up. Value the voices of those around you and empower them to bring their best.

Day 187

What that other leader is doing doesn't matter. How do they run their team is not important. What matters is what your team is doing and what your team needs. When you are worried about everyone else and what they are doing and what their opinions of you are, you are focused on yourself. That inward focus distracts you from those around you. And a disconnected leader is an ineffective leader.

The comparison game is deadly for leaders and your team culture. Copying another leader is inauthentic and ineffective. Focus on being the leader your team needs.

Day 188

A talented team with an unhealthy culture can win, but its success is limited. A team with no talent and unhealthy culture won't win. A team with some talent but a healthy culture will overachieve. A talented team with healthy culture is capable of greatness. And it's that culture that attracts talented players who fit into a great culture, creating not just a flash in the pan of success, but a program that lasts. Coaching plays a role, of course, but at some point even coaches cancel each other out. The great coaches are ones that know the game but spend just as much time cultivating a healthy culture.

Talent matters and coaching matters, but culture will ultimately determine a team's success. Great leaders create culture intentionally.

Day 189

You show up every day, doing what you've always done, but the results aren't coming. You say the things you've always said the way you've always said them. You give the same pitch. You do the same work. And it's just not working.

We can keep doing the same thing and be frustrated, we can simply give up and just show up without any skin in the game, or we can realize that there's a better way.

A new day calls for a new kind of leadership. A kind of leadership that is rooted in humility, that fights for the good of the team, that values what every person brings to the team. It won't be easy but it will be necessary.

In order to be a leader who makes a difference, you're going to have to do things differently.

Day 190

You share the vision, close the meeting and head to work. A week later, you're frustrated because nobody seems to know what's happening or where they're going.

So you call another meeting and remind them of the vision. A few blank stares and head nods that you mostly ignore, thinking surely this time they understand. A week later, everyone is going in different directions, working on their own things.

If you don't speak their language, communicate a clear and hopeful vision of the future and create a bridge of how you'll get there, you lose the members of your team. No matter how fired up you are, your message must resonate and connect with them if they are to act on it and build that future with you.

A leader who doesn't communicate well creates confusion and chaos, leading to a disconnected and unproductive team. Don't just speak. Be heard.

Day 191

Every time you turn on the news or open social media it feels exhausting. And this is coming from someone who loves and values social media. With our current political climate it feels like every day is another crisis, another battle, another argument.

As a citizen, it can feel overwhelming. As a leader, it can feel the same way. It can feel like the best option is to just not care, to go through the motions, to look out for our own interests. "If the world's going to hell in a hand basket, I might as well get mine." "What's the use anyway? Whatever is said is going to be debated and critiqued and it's just not worth it."

It is worth it. It's easier than ever to just give in and let the noise win.

Block out the noise. Focus on your team. Focus on the vision. Amidst the chaos, leaders bring clarity and create a culture where the team thrives.

Day 192

You have a couple of wins, hit a few goals, have a few good weeks."We're on a roll. We've got this thing figured out." This is a mindset many leaders face. A few things go our way and we settle into a position of comfort.

One of the greatest enemies of success is complacency. The second you think you have it figured out, chaos hits. You ignore the fundamentals, you let a few things slide, and suddenly those moments of success are undone.

This is where true leadership comes in. In moments of greatness, in moments of success, do you get comfortable or do you stay focused? Celebration is necessary, but that doesn't mean the work is done. The same behaviors that create success will sustain it.

Great leaders undermine their influence when complacency sets in. Creating healthy culture is a daily journey, not a destination.

Day 193

I had a boss in my early career who spent two mornings with me each month (roughly an hour each meeting) talking about life. He wanted to know how my marriage was, how my kids were doing, how fatherhood was impacting me. He challenged me in all of these areas (and others) to be better. To be married to my wife, not my work. To be present with my kids, not just be a provider for them. He had influence with me, which gave him permission to call me up to a higher standard in these areas.

I quickly realized that this wasn't normal boss behavior. None of my friends had experiences like this at work. The result? I loved my job and was committed to being great at it. Not only for myself, but for my boss and the team. He made me want to be better. He didn't force me to, but his leadership style made me want to step up. Most of my other friends just went to work. They went through the motions each day.

Everybody wants those they lead to be better at their roles. They want their salespeople to become great at sales, they want their point guard to take her skills to a new level, they want their marketing managers to be experts in their field. So we focus on their hard skills necessary to do their jobs. We focus on them as employees and role players. And we get people that play the role, that show up and just do the job.

The key to getting the most out of your team is to view its members as more than their positions. Call them up to greatness in life. To be great husbands and wives, fathers and mothers, community members and team members. Leaders build leaders.

Your job isn't to help your team be good at their roles. Your job is to help them become leaders worth following in every circle of influence.

Day 194

Fear might win today. Overpowering your team may get them to do the work you want and get the results you desire. Fighting for what you want might in fact get you what you want. Today.

Tomorrow, though? Tomorrow it won't work.

Over time, that approach loses. When we're for ourselves, we forget about those we lead. We forget about the impact our choices have on them. We forget that we are leading people. Our self-preservation turns our focus inward, rather than on those we lead. And as a result, we undermine our influence. Slowly but surely, the foundation we've built (that was shaky, at best) begins to crumble. Your team decides that not only don't people want to follow you, but they don't have to.

Results don't matter if we didn't help our team get better in the process. Winning doesn't matter if it came at the cost of your people and your influence.

Without influence, you've lost your ability to impact and lead.

Each day you have to make a choice: will you be for yourself or for your team?

Create a vision of hope, empower your team to believe it can be great and help it achieve it, fight for the highest good. Culture wins championships.

Day 195

Meetings are easy. Creating culture is hard. Working through your to-do list is easy. Creating culture is hard. Settling for the status quo is easy. Creating culture is hard. Serving your own interests is easy. Creating culture is hard.

Every day we're facing a battle. A battle of settling for what is versus fighting for what could be.

There is no shortcut to creating healthy culture. Most people won't do the hard, necessary work. Those who do will build not only build championship programs and organizations, they'll also build a legacy of success.

Day 196

Today, you will shape and create culture with the words you speak, the actions you take, the decisions you make, your body language, the work you do.

The question isn't whether or not you are creating culture; the question is are you doing it intentionally or accidentally?

Day 197

Insecure leaders attract insecure talent and build insecure teams that cater to the leader's insecurities.

Leaders without ego attract talent with no ego which leads to a team with no ego.

How you lead each day is 100% up to you. Leaders define culture.

Day 198

We don't realize the story each person brings to the table. We get such brief interactions that all we see of people is that very moment, ignorant to the life and years they've lived up to that point.

Imagine the stories of pain and success those on your team have. Do you know those stories? If not, you don't truly know your people. You don't know why they are the way they are, why they view the world the way they do, and how to effectively lead and empower them.

And a bigger point, do they know these things about you? You shouldn't be a mystery to your team. You shouldn't be an untouchable figure. They should know who you are and why you are. Let them in. A connected team is crucial for a championship culture.

Great culture doesn't happen without vulnerability and transparency. Know the individuals on your team and their stories, and let your team know you. Leaders go first.

Day 199

"What does my team want?" That's a question many leaders are trying to answer. They think if they give their team what it wants, everyone will buy in. If they give them what they want, they'll show up and work hard and have a good culture and the results will follow.

The problem is that what your team wants changes all the time. If you're chasing *want*, you'll never get there. It's a moving target.

What your team needs, though, is different. Your team members, no matter who they are and what they want, need to be heard. They need to be valued. They need to be supported and challenged. They need to be believed in. The good news? You can give them those things. You can listen to them. You can value them. You can support and challenge them. You can believe in them. You can fight for them. You can do that every day. The commitment and culture and results you want? They'll come when you show up focused on need rather than want.

Your job isn't to give your teammates what they want. Your job is to give them what they need (to be supported, challenged, believed in, valued).

Day 200

"This is terrible. How could you do this? I can't believe you made a mistake like this. I'm so disappointed. Get it fixed, immediately!"

"This is who you are right now, but this isn't who you have to be. Here's what I see in you."

Are you calling people out or are you calling people up? This mindset is a huge shift. Calling out is about us; calling up is about them. We have to ask ourselves, in these moments, what it's like to be on the other side of our leadership. Calling people out can feel like we're against them, calling up shows we're for them.

Rather than calling your people out, call them up. Remind, challenge and empower them to be the leader they are capable of being. Show you're for them.

Day 201

When my oldest son was almost 7, he was aggressive on the basketball court. He took control, drove to the basket, made good passes, took good shots, went for rebounds and always had his head in the game.

A year later, he was completely out of almost every game. Amped up before the game, he would hide when the whistle blew. When he had the ball, panic. Bad passes, awkward shots, poor decisions.

While I certainly don't expect perfection or anything close to it, I was concerned about the change and interested in what was going on, so I asked him. I made sure he knew I wasn't disappointed and that I didn't think he was doing anything wrong, but that I had noticed the change and was curious about what caused it to see if there was something I could do to help.

Through tear-filled eyes, he said that he was nervous. We kept talking (and I kept reinforcing that he'd done nothing wrong), and eventually it came out that he felt like everyone was watching him and that made him nervous and uncomfortable because he doesn't like to fail - especially in front of people.

We worked through the issue and he felt confident after we were done, and he was much more aggressive after that. I realized there was a lesson there for me, and for all of us.

Every day I wake up and my head is filled with fear and insecurities. Every single day. I wonder if people like me, if people trust me, if I can actually do the work I'm pouring my life into, if I'm good enough, if I'm going to do something today to bring it all crashing down.

If I ignore those fears, they grow. They eat at my mind throughout the day and they impact my performance. They result in me making poor decisions. They prevent me from being my best, for myself and for others. If I name them and acknowledge them, I can fight them with truth. The fear and lies and insecurities don't have to win.

What are you afraid of today? Name your fears in order to overcome them. Lead today being secure in who you are. Empower those you lead to do the same.

Day 202

I want my wife to know she's valued and appreciated. I want my boys to be confident yet humble, driven yet secure, compassionate and intentional. I want those I work with to know they are capable, to know they matter, to know the value they bring. I want the team to communicate well, to fight for each other, to say no to their ego.

My guess is you all want similar things in your life. You want to do work that matters and you want those near you to know they matter. You want a culture that people want to be a part of, a culture where people thrive.

So what are you doing to make that happen? What actions, what conversations, what plans can you put into place today?

Your team culture won't magically get better because you want it to. You have to show up each day and do the work. Hope isn't a strategy.

Day 203

"I just need him to be more of a vocal leader."

"She's great at what she does but I'm not sure she has that *it* factor. She never speaks up."

"I'm gonna need you to pick up your leadership a bit. Let's take it to the next level."

Quietness is not a weakness or a sign of a poor leader. In our culture, though, it's often the loud ones who get the platform, the promotion, the attention, the authority. There are times when we need to speak up but loudness is not leadership.

Leadership is made up of our actions, of our integrity, of our intent. Leadership is our ability to balance support and challenge. It is valuing and empowering every voice around the table or locker room to speak up. It is fighting for others. It is knowing when to speak up and when to listen and let others have the stage.

Leadership doesn't have to be loud. Show up, be great at what you do, have integrity and humility, speak up when necessary.

Day 204

Not money. Not recognition. Not promotions. Not titles. Not a health center. Not benefits.

Study after study shows that what employees (and you could replace that with team members, players, etc.) really want is to be valued. They want to believe the work they are doing matters and they want to know that those they work for are actually for them. Yet study after study also shows that 70% of people are not engaged in their work.

Where our mind goes, our actions go. If we're thinking about tasks and revenue and budgets, our actions follow. If we're thinking about helping our people becoming the best they can possibly be, our actions will follow.

If we aren't focused on our people, on creating a culture that builds leaders, we're focused on the wrong thing. Show up each day to fight for the highest good of those you lead.

Day 205

Your development team is getting better at raising funds. Your communication and marketing teams are getting better at telling your story. Sales are up. Online engagement is strong.

All of these are good things. These are signs of growth, the result of hard work. And, many times, the result of a focus on tasks.

Your people are getting better at their jobs but are they getting better as leaders? Do they simply show up to do decent work, or do they show up to truly contribute and bring their best each day? Are they communicating clearly, are they aware of their strengths and weaknesses (and how those strengths and weaknesses impact the team), are they raising the level of those around them?

The question for leaders is this: are we building more leaders?

Managers focus on tasks. They obsess about efficiency and KPIs and the bottom line. I became this way when I was in the corporate world. I was so focused on the numbers on our spreadsheets that I forgot there were people involved. And I hate spreadsheets. Even when we were growing, you could feel the tension and disconnect. Growth is not always the result of good, healthy leadership.

Leaders focus on people. They know that people make the culture and, if we invest in and empower our people, they not only become better leaders but they also become better at their jobs. It's in this environment that teams thrive.

Don't just help your people get better at their jobs. Help them become better leaders. Leaders worth following build leaders worth following.

Day 206

During a session with a college athletics marketing team, one team member mentioned some deep frustration with a someone in another department. Specifically, it was around a certain behavior that their team member consistently displayed. I asked if they had talked to the person about it. Blank stare. "Everyone in this room nodded their head, clearly aware of your frustration. Some of them may share the same frustration. Has anybody actually talked to this person about the impact his behavior is having on the team?" Again, blank stares.

Before the meeting was over, one person committed to approaching the "frustrating" team member about the issue.

A few weeks later I followed up, asking if they'd had the conversation and how things were going. "It's amazing! They had no idea their behavior was causing so much drama and they felt terrible about it. Now that they know it, they've changed. And it hasn't always been perfect, but when now when they act that way, they immediately notice it and apologize."

Crazy, isn't it? If we were the ones causing tension, we would want someone to let us know. And being the last one to know about your issue can be embarrassing. People want to get better. If you believe that, and if you also want them to get better, we'll learn how to challenge well in order to fight for their highest good - and the highest good of the team. The health of our culture depends on it.

The key in this is that people must know you're for them. If they don't respond well to challenge you must first check your intention. Are you for yourself, are you against them or are you for them? More often than not, people respond well to challenge when they trust the intent of the person bringing it. If they think you're trying to attack or demean them, they get resistant rather than responsive. Be clear, be positive, and help them see what it's like to be on the other side of them.

When your colleagues know you're for them, they're OK with being challenged and held accountable. They know you're fighting for their best.

Day 207

As I talk with leaders and interview leaders and study teams and organizations, I believe more and more that we are in the midst of a defining moment of leadership. For decades, leaders have operated a certain way because they could. They could be overpowering and demanding; they could be domineering and controlling. My parents and my grandparents weren't as concerned about the purpose behind the work they were doing. They were grateful to have jobs and careers and to be providing for their families.

None of that is to paint a doom-and-gloom picture of leadership. Certainly there were those doing great work, who cared about their people, who went beyond the status quo.

Today, though, is a different time. Today, leaders can still do what needs to be done to get by. Their teams might get results and they may think everything is okay.

Or, they can be worth following. They can get to know their people. They can realize that people are people and not items on a budget. They are more important than the work, more important than the bottom line.

And in my conversations, I feel this tension. There's a changing of the guard happening. And it's not necessarily from old leaders to young leaders, it's from an old leadership mindset to the new reality. Leaders are realizing the need to operate with a different mindset. That culture and values are not just talking points but daily actions. That we must not only be highly competent but have high character. If you ignore it, you'll undermine your influence. If you embrace it, not only will you win but those you lead will win. Your team, your organization, your family.

It isn't easy, it doesn't happen quickly, and it requires vulnerability and humility. But it is so worth it. So let's lay aside our pride, let's lay aside what we think we know, let's lay aside our fear, and let's do the hard work of becoming leaders worth following.

The leaders who succeed going forward will be those who do the hard work to understand their people and connect with them. Be that leader.

Day 208

Every day you show up and tell your team what to do. Finish this project. Create this document. Raise these funds. Run these drills. Launch that campaign.

You repeat the demands often. Everything is about the what. Everything is about the task. You get frustration when it isn't done to a certain standard or with a certain enthusiasm. The job is done but there doesn't seem to be buy-in.

The problem is your people don't know why. They don't know why this project. Why this document. Why these funds. Why these drills. Why this campaign. Why we do what we do, and why we do it a certain way. They are surrounded by the what. A world of information is just a click away. If you want commitment, if you want them to value and believe in the work they do, if you want them to do it with purpose, tell them the why. And repeat it every day.

The what may get boring but the why always matters. The why drives the what as well as the how.

Your team knows what to do but does it know why? The why breathes life into the what. Share it daily.

Day 209

You hit your monthly goals. You won the games you needed to win. You raised the funds you needed to raise. You hit your key metrics. Achieving goals is not always the result of great leadership. Bad leaders can get results. Leaders who lead out of fear can get results (for a time). Leaders who are incompetent but are lucky enough to have a talented team can get results (for a time).

We can't always measure success by goals we hit or don't hit. That's the easy way out and it results in a lot of bad leadership. Leaders worth following know that true success comes from both hitting goals and from the growth of their teams. It comes from the team being committed and connected, from all members knowing they played a role in and have ownership of the success, and from our people being better today than they were yesterday - not just our bottom line looking better.

Good leaders focus on goals. Great leaders focus on their people and end up achieving more than their goals. They build a program, not just a team.

Day 210

We all look at great teams, great organizations, great leaders and wish we could be like them. Sometimes that is out of unhealthy jealousy but many times we simply want to be great and be a part of a great team/organization. We're naturally drawn to greatness.

This is a topic that comes up in almost every one of our sessions. Most leaders want to be great. They want their teams to be great. Often I'll ask what they've done in the last day/week/month to be great, and what they've done in that time to help their team become great. It turns into a few moments of awkward silence. I then ask if their schedule has simply been dominated by tasks and to-do lists, completing the list of things that popped up on their calendar for that day. Heads nod.

The point isn't to make people feel bad. We're all in the same boat (the good news for them is that they realized it and asked for help). We all think about being great and about leading great teams, but that's typically all we do. Think and hope.

To be great, we have to act. To lead great teams, we have to act and create. We have to talk about the culture and create the culture. We have to talk about valuing people and we have to value people. We have to talk about empowering others and we have to empower them. Only then will we have a culture that not only develops great talent but attracts great talent, and guides that talent down the path to becoming a great team.

Great teams aren't great by accident. They create cultures everyone wants to be a part of and where everyone matters. Be intentional.

Day 211

Insecure leaders are overly demanding. They constantly change direction in order to keep control. They make a big deal out of insignificant things. They never hear the truth from their teams because those teams are afraid of what response they may get.

Secure leaders want greatness and support/empower their teams to achieve it. They focus on what's important — the people — in order to reach the goal.

Insecure leaders have teams that show up and operate out of fear. Secure leaders have teams that show up for each other. Leaders define culture.

Day 212

Examine how you lead each person on your team. We typically don't treat people the same (which is a good thing). Some on your team you micromanage. You hover over their every move, waiting for a mistake to correct. Others you are treat almost as if they can't do anything. You push and push and push and push. There are some on your team you are completely hands off; it may appear as though you've given up on them. And others you give both authority and responsibility. You empower them to do great work.

The question for each group or person is why? Why do you treat them the way you do? Typically, this goes back to our perspective of the person. How we feel about a person impacts how we lead them. And if we have a negative perception of a person, we have to look at a whole host of other issues.

It's on us to see what people are capable of and help them believe that as well. If we don't think they're capable of doing great work, we won't lead them to do great work and they'll never do great work.

If you trust those your team, you'll empower. If you're skeptical, you'll overpower, micromanage or abdicate. Believe in their potential and fight for them.

Day 213

Where are you going? Do you know? Do you think about it? Does your team know?

Some leaders don't think about the future or casting a vision. They focus on the task at hand for the day, so much so that there may appear to be no vision. Every day feels almost the same and there is no clear direction or purpose to the team's work. The work matters but your team must know why it matters and where it is leading.

Some leaders are almost solely focused on the future. They get so wrapped up in casting vision that they forget about the work that needs to get done today. They get impatient at the lack of immediate measurable results. Speaking about the vision doesn't magically make it happen.

Leaders worth following must balance both. They know that building culture is playing the long game. Know where you are going, know how to get there and communicate both to the team often.

Building culture is thinking about tomorrow and what must be done today to create it. It's worth the work. Culture wins championships.

Day 214

How do I want to be remembered?

As a husband, as a dad, as a leader, as a co-worker, as a friend. How do I want to be remembered? Do I want to be remembered as a workaholic, as a grouch, as lazy, as distracted, as inconsistent, as caring only about my interests? Or do I want to be remembered as someone who was for others, who made others better, who was intentional in work and life, who was trustworthy and compassionate? Do I want to be remembered as someone who just showed up or as someone who showed up with purpose?

If I can answer that question, I have a framework for how to approach each day and each interaction. From my conversations to my health, from my businesses to my family.

Most of us want to be remembered for great things. The problem is that we simply hope it happens. We live life accidentally, simply going through the motions. The reality is that who we are is up to us. And who we are is what we will be remembered for. Every day is an opportunity to choose who we want to be. Nobody can stop us. Nobody shoulders any blame but us.

So how do you want to be remembered? What actions will you take to make that a reality? Be intentional. Leave accidental living behind.

Day 215

I used to crave credit. I'd sit in on meetings and when someone mentioned how well a member of my team was performing, I would chime in with why my leadership was causing their success. "Yeah, I've been getting here early to coach her. She's responded really well." "I've been working on a plan with him. It's really showing." "I noticed this one thing he was doing that was causing problems in closing deals. Now he's doing it the way I suggested and his numbers are skyrocketing."

Isn't that disgusting? I was so insecure that I couldn't just let praise of my team be enough. I had to make sure that the leadership team knew that *I* was the one responsible for each success. What's even worse is that I'd spoken out against that behavior. "Let your work speak for itself. Don't beg for attention." Yet here I was, doing the very thing I hated (if we're honest, we find we do this often).

Leadership isn't about you. It's about the people you lead. It's about serving them, challenging them, developing them, empowering them. It's about putting them in positions to succeed and not needing any credit for their success. Knowing that those you lead have succeeded is the only reward you need.

Insecure leaders need credit, praise and attention. Secure leaders shine the spotlight on their team.

Day 216

Noah, our middle son, was scared to ride his bike. Typically fearless, he admitted he was afraid of falling. He had practiced a few times but now we were ready to really get after it. Gabe, our oldest, was the same way. Fear was crippling them (and, if I'm honest, frustrating me).

We had a little pep talk and they decided to give it another try. And they nailed it. They started without help, rode down the street and into a school parking lot where they did laps for 20 minutes. With each lap, confidence grew. They laughed, they smiled, they raced. "Dad, I'm doing it!"

It was amazing to see how comfortable they were. In a matter of a minutes, fear that had lasted most of the summer turned to joy, excitement, comfort.

On the other side of fear is confidence. And we look back and realize that, while our fear was real, we gave it too much power. We treated it like a mountain when it was really a pebble.

So what fears are holding you back as a leader? What conversations are you afraid to have? What decisions are you afraid to make? What visions are you afraid to pursue? And do you realize how that fear is also being passed down to your team (and family)?

Name it. Move into it. Defeat it.

Fear is a liar designed to keep you from making the impact you were created to make. Don't give it power over you today. Be bold, take action and watch your team do the same.

Day 217

Leadership is for "them." We're not sure who they are, but it's not me. You have to be "special" to be a leader. You have to have something different about you. You have to have the "it" factor. I'm just here to do my work.

Many of us think that way. We think leadership is reserved for a certain group and we convince ourselves that we aren't part of that group. What we're actually doing is giving ourselves an out. We're allowing ourselves to not take ownership, to not speak up, to not take action. If we're not a leader, it's not our job.

The beauty of leadership is that everyone gets to play. It's for AD and head coach and CEO. It's for the intern and the new guy. There is no selection committee, no admissions application, no form to fill out. You just have to pick yourself.

Leadership isn't for the extraordinary. It's simply for those who show up on purpose, with no ego, who want others to become their best. Be that person today. Jump in the sandbox and play.

Day 218

"I got comfortable. And because I was comfortable, the team became comfortable. Turns out, that's a dangerous thing for a team." While doing a leader intensive for an AD recently, this was one of his big aha moments.

Everything was going well. Teams were performing, more donors were giving more money than ever, projects were moving along. There were legitimate reason to celebrate.

And then he stopped challenging things. He started relishing in the success (not a bad thing) and took his eye off the ball. Meetings that regularly took place were cancelled. Collaboration that resulted in new ideas no longer was a priority. "We're good enough."

When slip-ups started to happen, they were ignored. Because they were ignored, growth stopped. Not just outwardly - in wins and fundraising and branding initiatives - but inwardly. Challenge leads to growth. And when we aren't challenged, we don't grow.

Unfortunately, it was too late to save - or that's what he thought. Rather than try to right the ship, he had taken a new position. It was only now, months later, that he was slowing down to think through what happened, to own his role in it, and realize that it actually could have been saved had he kept calibrating support and challenge.

Comfort leads to complacency which leads to stalled growth. The work of creating a championship culture is never done. Celebrate success, but keep moving forward.

Day 219

You won't read a book or listen to a podcast or attend a seminar or scan a blog post that will give you the answer for your culture. There are no 3 C's, 4 must have's, 5 key traits that you can simply install today and be good to go.

You can drive through and instantly have a full meal for you and your family. You can drive through and get your oil changed without ever leaving the car. From the comfort of the driver's seat, you can get drop off and pick up your laundry, get your prescriptions, grab a cup of coffee and a variety of other things.

At the tip of our fingertips we have access to every bit of information, every moment of breaking news, every score and highlight, and can order food, book travel, know when it's going to rain and deposit money into our bank accounts.

We live in a drive-through society of convenience, but there is no drive-through, convenient option for creating healthy culture. It takes time, perseverance and work. Show up.

Day 220

It's tough to try a different path, to lead out of our off hand, to connect with someone in a way that's unnatural to us but natural to them, to speak up instead of being silent. When we try, it's awkward. It's uncomfortable. It's frustrating.

Fear kicks in. Insecurity kicks in. Doubt kicks in. And we make excuses for why we should stop. We go back to the way things used to be and we settle for a frustrating, insufficient status quo.

The charge here is to not give up. To not stop. To not give in. Your culture is worth it. Your team is worth it. Your happiness and success are worth it. Your legacy is worth it.

Culture won't change in one meeting or overnight. It takes time. A long time. It takes perseverance and commitment. Show up on purpose.

Day 221

"What that team is doing looks like it's working. We should try that."

"Did you hear about what they did? Maybe we should look at doing that."

"They got a lot of buzz for this. Let's see if it works for us."

Visions and purpose can be like diet fads. We're always attracted to the next great thing that someone else is doing. While we can learn from what others are trying, we can't simply copy what they do.

The problem is that we undermine influence with our team because we can't commit to who we are or who we want to be. The goal posts keep moving and people don't know which way to go. Eventually they get tired of it, knowing that this direction is as temporary as the last one. You aren't committed, so they know they don't need to be either.

Your team is your team, not another team. It must have a unique vision and purpose, not a copycat vision.

When you don't believe in your story/purpose/vision, you'll easily be distracted by trying to live someone else's. Own your why.

Day 222

You can read the latest hot book on leadership but that isn't actually leadership.

You can listen to a podcast about leadership but that isn't leadership.

It's no surprise that there are thousands of books and blog posts and podcasts on leadership. It's a relevant topic and millions of people consume the content.

That's the easy part. I remember a few years back, when I was running a failed company, I would sit and read leadership and creativity blogs all day. I was convinced that I was leading and creating and producing. I realize that sounds ridiculous but it's unfortunately true.

Who was I leading? Nobody. Why in the world would anyone follow someone who consumed leadership content all day yet didn't actually lead?

Doing those things isn't bad. Leaders are learners and books, blogs and podcasts are great ways to learn. But what good is that knowledge if we don't use it? That's accidental leadership.

What you know doesn't make you a leader, it's about what you do. Leading is a verb. Take action today. Lead intentionally.

Day 223

You have the right goals. You have the best processes and systems in place. You have the right vision and way forward. You even have talented people.

All of that can be undone if you've not invested in your people and created a healthy culture.

The right people will miss the right goals in an unhealthy culture. The right people will never make the right vision a reality in an unhealthy culture. The right processes and systems will be useless in an unhealthy culture.

Leadership and culture building are about people. They are your greatest assets. Make them your highest priority and invest in them daily.

Day 224

A positive leader will have a positive team. An angry leader will have a fearful team. A hopeful leader will have a hopeful team. A passive-aggressive leader will have a gossipy team. A moody leader will have an unstable team.

Leadership is contagious. What kind of attitude, culture, mindset are you passing on to your team?

Day 225

We all want a healthy culture, and we want it now, but few are willing to put in the work to create it. It's too hard or it's somebody else's job or we don't know the first step. So we complain, we gossip, we get lost in our tasks. And tomorrow we do the same thing. And nothing changes.

Don't make excuses for your team's culture not being what it should be. Create it. Today. It starts with you.

Day 226

Will you be for yourself today or will you be for others?

Will you take ownership of your leadership or will you blame others?

Will you be present, connected and build the culture your team deserves or will you hope it happens?

Will you lead with humility today or will pride win?

Will you fight through self-preservation or will fear drive your decisions today?

Will you listen to others from their perspectives or will you view them incorrectly through your own lens?

Would you want those you lead to model how you live today? Be worth following.

Day 227

When things are stressful, when numbers are down, when losses are piling up, this is when many people start to think about their team culture. It's natural. It typically takes pain for a leader to make changes. I always thought about and talked about leadership, but it was only when I felt the pain of burned bridges and undermined influence did I realize I had to act. I could continue down a road of pride and self-preservation, or I could become the leader I wanted and needed to be.

I'm not there yet and may not ever be, but I'm closer than I was two years ago and I'm closer than I was yesterday. Awareness and improvement.

Yet great leaders focus on culture at all times. It's easy to get lazy when things are good but that is when the seeds of unhealthy culture can be planted. You let this conversation slide, you avoid that needed moment of accountability and before long entitlement sets in. As stress hits, those seeds of unhealthy culture begin to grow. Once they take hold and extreme stress hits, we start to think about culture again.

If we think about, communicate and build on our culture daily, we can avoid the moments of extreme stress that tears apart teams.

Culture must be reinforced during the good times, not just seen as a remedy when things are down. Make it a daily focus.

Day 228

You sit down, turn on your computer and you are overwhelmed. A meeting at 8:00, a conference call at 9:15, an operations meeting at 10:00, brainstorming with the team on a project over lunch, and on and on. Rinse and repeat the next day and the next. If we aren't careful, it's easy for us to get lost in our work. A phrase I hear daily from leaders is, "I just don't have time. I'm too busy." We're all busy. We live in an always on world. It's not going to get easier.

Your people, though, they need you. They need to hear from you, to connect with you, to be encouraged, supported and challenged by you. They see you, they hear from you in meetings, but there's no real connection taking place. Eventually they decide to just focus on their work and ignore those around them. A disconnected leader creates a disconnected team.

Make time for them. If you value you them, you'll find the time. It's there. The rest of the work isn't going anywhere but your team might (physically or mentally). The investment in people is worth it. Don't hope it happens, make it happen.

Accidental leaders get distracted by their to-do lists. Intentional leaders stay focused on creating a culture people want to be a part of.

Day 229

All of us can get better at our jobs. We can always improve, there's always something to learn, always a better way to do what we do. If we care about our work and those around us, we'll want to get better. Too often, this is all leaders focus on. They want their team to be more efficient, more talented, more productive.

At some point, there's a diminishing return. We have to look beyond talent to character. We have to help those we lead become leaders. We have to help them become people that others want to work with, people that others want to follow. This is a crucial difference in managers and leaders. Managers care about how good their team members are at doing their jobs. Leaders care about how the team can connect, thrive and become an unstoppable unit.

Great leaders develop the character of their teams, not just their talent. Teams with great character are connected, committed and successful.

Day 230

Talented people without character will destroy a team. They may be the best at what they do, but they'll do it for themselves, not for the good of those around them. Their pride and ego (which are really insecurity) keeps others from trusting them.

On the flip side, average talent with great character can thrive. Those people work for the good of the team, don't care about the credit and do what they can to raise their production to the level of those around them. They want to be better because they know it helps the team. People trust them, have patience with them, and want to work with them.

The best teams, of course, know that a healthy culture attracts talented people. And it's in this environment that teams are capable of achieving their best. Talent without ego works to make everyone around it better, without caring about credit or accolades. It makes others want to be better.

In a healthy culture, talent thrives. In an unhealthy culture, it gets undone by drama and insecurity. Culture wins championships.

Day 231

Something is missing. Your team knows what to do, and folks show up every day to do their jobs, but something is off. You call another meeting, communicate the vision again, rally the troops and send them out, yet something just doesn't seem right. Nobody is bickering, nobody seems to be outwardly fighting, but nobody seems to be working together. Nobody seems to be working for the person next to him. Nobody seems fully bought in. They know it, but they don't *know* it.

You have to make the vision relevant to those you lead. They have to know how it benefits them, not just how it benefits you. Make it personal, make it connect. To do that, you have to take the time to know your team beyond "How was your weekend?" small talk. *Know* them. Know their hopes and insecurities, their talents and their weaknesses. Then show them how they can bring their best every day, why that matters, why you care, and what that does for them and the team.

Leaders don't give orders and pep talks. They build relationships and cast a vision that empowers their people to bring their best each day.

Your team may know the vision, but do they fully believe it? Leaders go for the heart, not just the head. Know your team to lead your team.

Day 232

Today you will be tempted to do what's best for you. You'll want to do what's best for your resumé, for your image, for your ego. It's not that you'll want to do it, but the temptation will be there. And it is an easy trap to fall into. It's in the DNA of work in America. Our work is who we are, so we design a way for us to win.

Leaders worth following fight the tendency to put themselves first. They look to serve the team, to do what's best for the team. At times, that might even come at a cost to them. The reward for that sacrifice? You become someone people want to follow. You become a leader that people want to work for because they know you'll fight for them. They know they can trust you. They know you are for them.

Your ego will take you out by convincing you to do what's right for you. Humility creates true success as you lead for the good of others.

Day 233

You will screw up today. You will fail someone. You will make the wrong decision. You may even make someone upset. Unless, of course, you don't try.

You have the choice to do nothing today. To abdicate your responsibility. To not step up. To not speak up. To not lead. To not try.

Sure we may fail if we try, but we'll also grow. We don't get better if we don't try. It's a guarantee that nothing gets better. We embrace the status quo if we just go through the motions. Nobody wants to be a part of that kind of culture.

Leadership takes courage. Courage to step up and courage to keep going when we fall. Show up and fight through fear today.

Day 234

When I first started Fieldhouse Media, I was amazingly insecure and immature. Every time someone would criticize me, or suggest my ideas weren't good enough, or that I wasn't experienced enough, I would lose it. It would cut right to my core. "Don't they know what I've done? I can't let this slide, it'll ruin everything I've worked for. If I don't defend myself, every single person in college athletics will think this criticism is fair." I laugh now at the absurdity of it. So I'd fire off a tweet or a blog post (the very thing I suggested not doing in our sessions with players, coaches and staff), throwing shade at the critics and defending myself. The amount of time I wasted in these meaningless battles is depressing to consider. And the reality? They did nothing but damage my reputation and distract me from the vision.

I had nothing to prove, yet I kept trying to prove myself. I had nothing to lose, yet I acted like I was about to lose everything. The only people I needed to worry about were the clients we were serving. Were they happy with the impact we provided? If yes, keep going and keep getting better. Period. Outside voices didn't matter. The only battles that matter are the ones that get us closer to the vision.

People see through insecurity. They see through pride. They see through immaturity. And the very thing you're trying to over-protect, you end up losing or severely damaging. There are battles worth fighting, for sure. Fight for the good of your people; fight for the good of your industry.

Insecure leaders waste time fighting every battle. Secure leaders fight the right battles. Wisdom breeds discipline which breeds credibility, which breeds influence.

Day 235

There is no guarantee of success. There will be bumps in the road. There will be mishaps. There will be failures. We are imperfect people leading other imperfect people in an imperfect world. And it is in these obstacles that our culture truly takes over. Will we default to our insecurities and fears, or will we press on for the good of ourselves and those around us? Will we be overtaken by the pressure or will we see the challenge as an opportunity?

A healthy culture doesn't guarantee an easy path. It determines whether obstacles will be a part of your story or the end of the story.

Day 236

Every year on January 1, millions of people decide they are going to get healthy. Few actually become healthy. How many people decide this is the year that they'll go for their dream, yet are still sitting in a cubicle in the corporate world?

In the same way, many of us want to be leaders. We may have even decided that we'll be leaders, or if we are in leadership positions, we've decided that we'll be better leaders. Yet if we look at ourselves honestly, our actions have not changed. Decisions without actions are empty promises.

Deciding to be a leader worth following doesn't make us one. We have to do what leaders worth following do. Take a step today.

Day 237

Is the culture in your department what you want? If we're honest, most of us would say it isn't. Even if it's good, it most likely isn't where we want it to be or where it could be. The question is how you respond to that. Do you criticize and gossip about how the "leaders" aren't fixing it? Or maybe you walk around telling people the way things should be? What, though, are you doing to make it better? What are you doing to own your role, to step up, to care, to act?

We can talk about the culture, complain about the culture or create the culture. Commit to making things better today.

Day 238

You don't have to lead the way your old boss did. You don't have to lead the way your mom or dad did. You don't have to lead the way your coach did. And you don't have to lead the way the person down the hall does, or the person in that other organization that everyone talks about.

The only person stopping you from becoming worth following is you. You get to decide the way you lead. What will you do today to live into that truth?

Day 239

You want your team to have a culture of humility, but are you leading with humility?

You want your team to have a positive culture, but are you leading with positivity, even during stressful times?

You want your team to have a culture of open communication but are you creating open channels of communication?

You want your team to have a culture of empowerment, but are you overpowering them?

When working with leaders, especially those who are stressed, I've almost always found a disconnect between the culture they want and the way they are leading. They are waiting for culture to change without leading that change. They are talking about it, but not living it.

The culture you want for your team must be created, not hoped for. It must be lived, not just discussed. Leaders set the tone. Lead intentionally.

Day 240

You can show up today and work. You can simply get the job done and do it well. You can acknowledge your co-workers and participate in meetings. You can live your normal routine, settling for the status quo. You might be productive, and your team might be as well.

Or you can show up today and fight for the highest good of the people next to you. You can support and challenge them to be better than they imagined. You can work for a vision that's larger than yourself, you can go beyond surface level conversations and actually know your team.

One way is easy and will probably get the job itself done. The other is harder, but creates an environment where teams reach heights they didn't know they were capable of. It requires intentional leadership.

You don't have to care, don't have to encourage, don't have to empower. But imagine what your team would be like if you did.

Day 241

Frustrated that your people are not doing the work you expected? Ask yourself if you defined your expectations or just assumed they knew what you wanted. Wondering why your team just doesn't seem to be on the same page when it comes to pursuing the vision? Ask yourself if you have communicated the vision clearly and often.

Too often we look to blame our team when the issues really start with us. If we can own our role and lead intentionally, we can begin to change the culture. Communicate it and live it.

Culture begins with you. Leaders define culture daily - with both their words and actions.

Day 242

Your culture is what people feel when they walk into the office in the morning. It's the way they feel when they go home and when they talk about work to their friends and family. It impacts they way they work, the way they interact. It empowers them to dream up ways the team can get better or it causes them to accept things as they are. It allows them to speak up or it causes them to simply put their head down and work.

Your culture is either breathing life into your team or it is suffocating them. Own it, define it, create it intentionally.

Day 243

You failed at your last job. You blew up and lost your cool and it cost you with your team. You never recovered from it and eventually left. Or maybe you sat silently as the culture deteriorated and you wear that guilt still.

You screwed up today. You think you'll screw up again tomorrow. You feel like every day is a challenge, every decision is second-guessed, every idea filled with doubt. You're not sure if you can regain momentum, for yourself or for the team.

It may not feel all doom and gloom, but it certainly feels stressful and doubtful. Insecurity creeps in.

I'm right there with you. Every day, I wake up and feel the attacks of fear and doubt. But I don't have to believe them. And I don't have to let them control how I live and lead. Our stories are part of us but they do not define whom we become. Yesterday's failure was yesterday. It only impacts today because we let it.

Our past and our present don't define the kind of leader we are. It's a choice. Decide to be a leader others want to follow, then live it.

Day 244

You can get what you want today by using fear. By bullying your way through conversations, convincing people to give in. Truthfully, you can even do this for a long period of time. You'll get your way often and you'll find few people speak up against you. They simply fall in line so that they don't get blown up. You'll convince yourself that they like you or trust you, that you have influence over them, but you don't. You have temporary influence, and permanent fear. Eventually this will catch up to you. It's not a place you want to end up.

You can also get what you want by helping others get what they want. By listening, communicating, compromising. By knowing their hopes and dreams and helping to make those reality. By sharing a vision people want to be a part of, a vision that helps everyone get better. There will be healthy debates, respected differences, and mutual commitments. People will listen to and follow you because they want to. This is true influence. Influence that lasts, that changes everything.

You can have temporary influence by overpowering others, or build lasting influence by empowering others. Will you lead with fear or hope today?

Day 245

Do you nitpick the work your team does? Are you quick to point out what was wrong before acknowledging what went well? Have you created an environment where people no longer speak up when they have an idea because they know you'll criticize it and ultimately shoot it down? In the midst of stress and tasks and busy seasons, it can be easy for us to default to being the critic. And at times, work certainly needs to be challenged in order to bring growth.

Don't let the stress of the day control you. Be intentional to challenge your team, support your team, encourage your team, dream with your team.

Leaders don't criticize their teams; they champion them. They call them up, not out. Create a culture you would want to be a part of.

Day 246

Everyone matters.

Everyone gets to play a part.

Everyone deserves to be heard.

These are all nice sayings that managers and "leaders" spout off as rallying cries, but what would happen if we actually believed them and lived them out? As leaders, it can be easy to write off the person who, in your mind, isn't contributing. As you push on toward the vision, he simply gets left behind. As you focus on the A players, the C players become D players. Eventually they're so disconnected that they simply show up because they have to. "Everyone matters," doesn't sound so good or so real to them.

Leaders see the potential in others, not just the skills they lack. It's on us to help them believe they can get from a 4 to an 8, and to give them the resources, opportunities, challenge and encouragement to make that happen.

As you press on toward your goal, don't leave people behind. Create a culture where you don't just say everyone is important, you actually live it out.

Day 247

You woke up and checked email. Immediately, your mind is focused on work. Driving to the office you're thinking about that one email you read that bothered you. Your drive to work could be a time for you to clear your head and mentally be ready for the day. Instead you're distracted.

You walk in the office and your mind is on your 9:00 meeting. You walk right past your team, offering no greeting. If you do happen to acknowledge them, it's without making eye contact or engaging. Your mind is on the meeting.

As the day goes on, emails pile up. More meetings come and go. Projects demand your attention. You may talk to your team but you aren't really with them. Even in meetings with the team, your mind is in another place.

Sound like you? This is the task-dominated life that most of us lead. We go through our days, shifting from one task to the next. We talk to our team but we don't engage them. We may look like we're listening but our mind is anywhere but in the meeting. We're living and leading a distracted life.

A distracted leader is a disconnected and ineffective leader. Learn to be present, to put people before tasks and ideas.

Day 248

Are you doing leadership to your people or with your people? When you're doing leadership to your team, they often feel like you're for yourself. Everything can appear to be about you. It's a quick way to have a disconnected and disengaged team.

When you do leadership with your team, they feel like you are for them. Everyone gets to play, everyone knows and agrees with the mission, everyone feels valued.

Leadership done to a team creates employees. Leadership done with a team creates more leaders. Be for your team today, not for yourself.

Day 249

You are a leader. The person next to you is a leader. The people down the hall are leaders. Same for those across campus and on the other end of the phone.

Do you believe you're a leader? Do they believe they are? Are you helping those around you believe they are leaders? Are we, as leaders, pursuing our best? Are we setting the standard and empowering others to be their best?

The world doesn't need more leaders, we need better leaders. We need leaders worth following. Show up today intentionally.

Day 250

When was the last time you talked with your team with no agenda? No plan, no purpose other than to sit, to talk, to listen.

If you don't listen to them, you won't understand them. If you don't understand them, you can't lead them. Leaders are listeners.

Day 251

Leaders sacrifice. They make decisions that don't always benefit themselves but do benefit those they lead. Leaders who sacrifice create teams that sacrifice. They'll work for the good of those next to them, at times sacrificing their own dreams and needs. Leaders who work for themselves create teams that work for themselves. When stress hits, everyone turns inward instead of fighting for the good of the whole.

Ego is a direct threat to your personal and organizational culture. Call it out, get rid of it and fight for the highest good of those you lead.

Day 252

Culture builds up or it tears down. It drives a team or holds it back. It will make or break you. It is hard to grasp, yet easy to explain. It is why your people show up or why they're looking to leave. It is being created accidentally or intentionally. It must be defined, created and protected. It must be constantly communicated.

Culture wins championships.

Culture is not a buzzword. It is what separates good teams from great teams. Leaders define culture.

Day 253

Many people don't want to be leaders; they want titles for the sake of power. They want the authority, the prestige, the control. It becomes a game of what you can get from others. It's the path of least resistance when it comes to being a leader.

True leadership is not about power, it is about influence. Where power seeks to take, influence is about giving. It's about others, not yourself.

Power comes from titles, influence comes from the way you lead. Leaders worth following use their influence to empower.

Day 254

To whom are you trying to prove yourself? What if they finally sent a note or made a call, giving their approval? Are you suddenly done? Is there nothing to work for anymore? Will the validation of your dad, your old boss, your current boss, make a real difference in the way you live and work? When we break it out that way, it sounds ridiculous. Of course we would still show up tomorrow and give our best effort. And we would do the same the next day, and the day after that. We spend our lives trying to prove ourselves, and it's exhausting.

The approval of others will not make you a better leader. Leave that pressure behind and show up every day for your team. Live and lead with nothing to prove.

Day 255

Culture is this odd, mysterious, often seemingly out of reach thing, isn't it? It can be hard to describe; it can be hard to nail down just exactly what it is. Is it our purpose? Is it our vision? Is it our strategy? Is it our environment? The way we treat each other? Is it our record (wins and losses, revenue and profit, goals hit)?

Yes, culture is all of that. And while it can be difficult to explain, we certainly know what it feels like to be part of a bad culture and what it feels like to be part of a good culture. We know when we've come to work because we have to and when we've come to work because we want to (even when, personally, we're having a bad day or season).

The results of culture are measurable. Increased or decreased communication, production, synergy, alignment, capacity, relationships. Culture wins championships.

Culture is too significant to ignore. Don't hope it happens — make it happen. Leaders define culture. Invest intentionally.

Day 256

Why. Vision. Strategy. Hiring. Promotions. Messaging/branding. Internal communication. Collaboration. Sales. Production. Meetings. Morale. Chemistry. From the cleaning crew to the receptionist to the star player to the CEO's office.

Culture touches it all. Culture is giving life to those people and roles and ideas, or it is bringing them down. It can at times be difficult to define and measure, but the importance of culture cannot be overstated.

Culture affects every person in every department, and impacts every decision that is made in a team and organization. Culture wins championships.

Day 257

Working with an organization recently, one of our sessions started at 9:00 and the boss showed up at 8:45. One of the senior leaders mentioned to me, "Wow. I'm surprised he's here this early. He typically shows up an hour late." After a bit of conversation, it was revealed that this boss is never on time, usually strolling in whenever he feels like it. I stored that away for later.

During our session, it became clear that he was an extremely demanding boss, with very high expectations of his team. Be on time, be prepared, go above and beyond, etc.

In our sessions, we try to create a safe environment for team members to speak up (and how well this plays out is certainly a direct reflection of the culture), and eventually someone finally broke. I had made a statement about leaders going first, about leadership starting with self. "If we don't hold ourselves to the same standards as those we lead, we undermine our influence. What do you think it's like to be on the other side of your leadership, if you are demanding one thing while doing the opposite?" Conversation started flowing and real breakthroughs started happening.

This boss walked away realizing how pride and complacency had settled in, and how he had unintentionally lost influence on the team. We created an action plan to get it back (this can't happen without the leader being self-aware and open to feedback - kudos to him for exhibiting these qualities. He was able to look in the mirror and realize what was happening.). Our last report showed a drastic turnaround, and tension around the department has decreased.

This situation could be playing out in millions of organizations and teams today. It's incredibly common.

Look at what you demand of others. Are you demanding the same from yourself? Leadership begins with you. You can't lead others well if you don't first lead yourself.

Day 258

"This will never work." "We can't go that direction." "We don't have the money/time/people to make that happen." "When this fails, we're done for." "We need to go back to the way things used to be."

"There will be hurdles but we can get over them." "When necessary, we'll adjust." "Each person on the team has something to bring. If we can get them to bring their best, anything is possible." "This is worth pursuing and, if it doesn't work, we'll learn, be OK and be better moving forward." "There's an opportunity for us to grow, to get better, to pursue more. Are you ready?"

These are two distinctly different leaders — one who is stuck in the past, one who is ready to move forward. One who is overly critical, one who is optimistic. To be clear, there is a time for questioning the plan. If we don't question it, we can't clarify it. And the plan may in fact not be worth pursuing. But if the response is always criticism, always resistance, always about staying put? That's detrimental to the team.

Cast a vision for what tomorrow could be, create a clear plan, and move toward a better tomorrow. Worry retreats; hope moves us forward.

Day 259

Insecure leaders yell and push back when they are questioned. They interrupt, they threaten, they tear down. They claw and fight to get their way, often at the expense of others. Their plans, words and goals always come back to what is best for them (often masked and sold as what would be good for others).

Secure leaders listen. They take challenges to their ideas as an opportunity to learn, refine and adjust. They are willing to change because, ultimately, they are for empowering those around them.

Question your intentions today. Are you fighting for your team or yourself? True leadership is about fighting for the highest good of those you lead.

Day 260

Fear tells you that you'll never be the leader your team/family/organization needs. Fear tells you that the hard work isn't worth it, to just stick with the status quo. Fear tells you that you can't get better, that your shortcomings aren't something you can overcome. Fear focuses on the negative.

The truth is that you aren't who you will be but you are enough. The truth is if it wasn't hard, it wouldn't be worth it. The truth is if you know yourself, you can lead yourself. Your weaknesses can be less of a liability. Being a leader worth following is a noble, worthy pursuit. Stay the course.

If we let it, fear and insecurity can overwhelm a leader. When you know your why, you can push through the self-doubt and have the strength to help others do the same.

Day 261

I played basketball growing up. To get better, I spent hours in the driveway practicing. When the whistle blew, I would put to use all of the things I had been practicing. Afterwards, I'd get back to work on the things that didn't go well, and refine those that did. Most sports are the same way. Practice in private or with a team, go execute in a game situation, then come back and practice in private.

Leadership, unfortunately, is not that easy. The game is our practice. It involves speaking up with real people, apologizing to real people, empowering real people. There is no private moment to work on it. All of our attempts, our success and failures, are public. When it gets awkward or we screw up, many leaders give up. It's too hard, it's too uncomfortable. The only way to grow, to become a leader worth following, is to push through the painful moments. It is in those moments that we get better, that our people see we are truly for them, that we are putting them first. It may not always be perfect, but the effort, and the heart behind the effort, will build influence.

Don't run away from the public, uncomfortable moments of leadership. If we can fight through them, we learn what we are truly capable of.

Day 262

Power is intoxicating. It makes us want things we've never wanted, think things we've never thought, do things we'd never do, say things we'd never say. It can turn humble people proud, secure people insecure, grateful people greedy. Self-preservation can kick in and we do whatever we can to keep that power. People that others once gravitated to, suddenly wonder where everyone went.

But it doesn't have to be that way. To gain a position of power, you were humble, you were secure, you were confident. You put others first, you were a team player, you were appreciative. Those things still matter. Now, more than ever.

Too many leaders do a 180 once they're in a position of power. The traits that got you there will also keep you there. Be worth following.

Day 263

The vision, the goal, the future. They all matter, but too many of us just focus on the vision. A vision without a plan to get there is just a dream. It's a hope. And hope isn't a strategy. Ideas are the easy part. Execution is what separates great leaders and teams.

Tomorrow's great results are a result of today's habits. You have the vision, but do you have the process and plan to get your team there?

Day 264

Winning is not everything. There is always something else to win. You'll never be satisfied.

Awards are not everything. There is always another award or achievement to pursue. It will never be enough.

Titles are not everything. Someone will always have a better title than you at a bigger/better organization. You'll always be climbing.

Serving people is everything. There is always someone who needs encouraged, inspired, empowered. It will never stop being rewarding.

Day 265

Asking for help is not a weakness; it is a strength. Being transparent and vulnerable with people is not a weakness; it's a strength. Taking time for yourself is not weakness; it is strength.

I know because I've been on the wrong end of this. I've gone too hard, too fast and too alone and I've ended up with anxiety and stress and paranoia and anger and everything in between. For others it leads to depression and worse. I have friends who have experienced it and friends who are experiencing it. Friends who are good people, good leaders pursuing good visions and dreams. Nobody is immune to it.

You have to be willing to fight for yourself, and surround yourself with people who will fight for you - and you have to allow them to fight for you.

Leadership can be exhausting and isolating. Make rest a priority and find people with whom you can be open with. Don't fight the fight alone.

Day 266

After snorkeling in Mexico, a friend brought up a point. "Even though we weren't in deep water and could see the bottom, it's fascinating to think about what was happening on the ocean floor that we couldn't even see. So much was going on that we were absolutely clueless about."

There were so many big fish and things near the surface that caught our attention, but we were unaware of all that was going on below. And without proper equipment, we truly couldn't know. But it was OK. We were concerned with the bigger picture.

Some of us as leaders, some of us can have a tendency to overly concern ourselves with the everyday minutiae. We want to be involved in everything, but that's really a mask for being controlling and micromanaging. It tells others we don't trust them. That we'll give them responsibility but not authority. You can be aware of what's going on but do you really need to be involved?

The details matter, but we can't lead our team toward the bigger picture if we're neck deep in details. Your team is capable of handling it. Low control, high accountability.

Leaders who are stuck in the day-to-day details will struggle to see the bigger picture. Cast a vision and allow your people to create it. Trust them. Empower them.

Day 267

Do you stand up for your team or do you always take the easy out that makes you look good but ends up hurting others? Do you look out for what's best for them or are you pursuing your own agenda? It can even be easy to convince ourselves (and try to convince others) that you're really looking out for them, when your actions clearly show otherwise - believe me, I've been there.

When we're constantly pursuing our own success at the cost of others, we ultimately end up losing. Community is everything and if others don't feel like we're for them, we'll lose them. Personal success is a tempting yet costly pursuit for a leader. We ultimately succeed by empowering others.

If you don't think your people are worth fighting for, you'll find they won't think you're worth following. Be for people.

Day 268

Think of the vision you have for your team for the next month, six months, one year, five years. Is it reasonable or does it seem crazy? Is it hopeful or realistic? We're living in a culture where, when a leader shares a hopeful, positive, beyond reason vision for the future, we label them unrealistic. "They're living in a dream world. That's just totally unreasonable to consider. They're an idealist."

Don't you want to follow an idealist? Don't you want to follow someone who has an amazing, hopeful vision for what tomorrow could be? Don't you want to shoot for 100 and hit 75 rather than shoot for 30 and hit 25? What seems ideal can become real.

We need leaders who dream big, positive, seemingly unrealistic dreams. Leaders who have the courage to go for it and who empower their teams to be better than they imagined.

Day 269

Whether it is for social media training of student-athletes and staff, or doing leadership development with athletics departments, I travel a lot. It should come as no surprise that Google Maps is one of my favorite and most-used apps. As I travel the country, Google not only shows me where I am but where I'm going and what issues could come up on the way. When traffic hits, Google gives me a way around it. If there's construction, Google finds a new path for me to take.

I've come to realize leadership is a lot like Google Maps. We can't move forward until we know where we are. Look around and assess the situation. Have enough self-awareness to recognize your own strengths and weaknesses. Now, where are we going? What are we working toward? Why? And is this just some grand vision or is there actually a plan for how to get there?

Empower your team to play a part in developing the plan. Now as we move forward, we all know where we are going and why, and we are comfortable making necessary shifts in the plan because we can see how they get us closer to where we're going.

Leadership is about the why, the what and the how. Leaders are clear about the now, have vision and direction for tomorrow, and the ability to adjust when necessary.

Day 270

In a recent conversation with a leader the topic of Pokemon Go came up (stick with me). While he thought it was ridiculous, I countered with the positives I had seen. "I don't claim to understand it or necessarily promote it, but I see kids exploring their neighborhoods and cities instead of sitting in front of a TV, and I see families spending time together exploring." The night before, I had actually passed a family I know, and all four of them were walking through a part of OKC searching for Pokemon (I still don't fully know what that means). They were spending time together. Laughing, exploring, engaging. It was really cool to see. The leader responded that he hadn't considered that aspect of it.

What does this have to do with leadership?

We're afraid and/or skeptical of things we don't know. Is your team afraid and/or skeptical of you because its members don't know you? Let them in and watch influence increase.

Day 271

You walk into work today and you immediately shift into automatic, working through your to-do list. You look up and it's 5:00, or later. What did you actually do today? Did you stop to encourage your teammates? Did you take a few minutes to invest in them? Did you remind them of what the goal is and why? Did you encourage their natural strengths and help them get better at their weak spots?

It's easy to go through our day being dominated by tasks. Leaders worth following make time to pay attention to others. Shift your mindset, change your culture.

Day 272

Can we just be honest about the fact that creating a healthy culture is hard? We all have insecurities and negative tendencies. The same is true of the people we're leading. As much as we want to do the right thing, we all tend to fall back into unhealthy behaviors (especially under stress and when trying to implement something new and meaningful is met with resistance). It won't happen overnight. It won't happen next month, it might not happen this year.

Yet study after study reveals that people would rather have a better boss than a pay raise. That the relationships with those they work with is what truly impacts their job satisfaction. That an unhealthy culture has a negative impact on their mental and physical health.

As leaders, we can't sit idly by. We can't hope for the best, we have to create it. I don't know who said it first but I'm always drawn to the quote, "What if we invest in our people and they leave? Well, what if we don't invest in them and they stay?"

Now more than ever we need leaders who are courageous. Who will fight to create the right culture for their team. It's a difficult but worthy fight.

Day 273

When working with teams and leaders, the conversation almost always starts with something that someone else is doing wrong. The leader is frustrated with their team, the team is frustrated with their leader, teammates are frustrated with each other. They almost always come into sessions with the hoping that the person frustrating them will have a magical "aha" moment that "fixes" the frustrating behavior.

To their dismay, one of the first things we tell teams and leaders to do is look in the mirror. Do you see the broccoli in your teeth? That thing you do that frustrates your team and peers and undermines your credibility?

While we're focused on others, we tend to ignore our own weaknesses and blind spots. And a leader who ignores her blind spots is a leader who will get taken out by them. When each person on the team looks within and realizes their opportunity for growth, teams start to truly come alive.

Leaders worth following don't try to "fix" their teams. They first look in the mirror and ask how they can get better. Lead yourself before you lead others.

Day 274

How many times have you shared the vision with your team, only to lose your credibility because you didn't execute? After so many times, people stop buying in. The result is a disengaged team and a frustrated leader.

"What? So what? Now what?" Leaders build credibility when they show up with the answers to those three questions. Vision must lead to intentional action.

Day 275

"I'd love to do something for my team, but there just isn't time." Imagine if your team heard you saying that. Imagine your boss or coach or parent saying that. How excited would you be to show up each day? If you don't have time to help your team get better, you don't have time to lead. You're simply showing up every day, making sure people are doing their work. It's a fast track to being a leader people have to follow rather than a leader people want to follow. If you won't invest in them, someone else will. The work matters but the people come first.

Leaders worth following show up each day believing their team are worth the investment. Empower their hopes, dreams and abilities. Fight for their highest good.

Day 276

Those on your team will show up because it's their job, because they are expected to, because they get paid. They will do great work because they are valued, because they are empowered, because they have a why they can commit to.

Any leader can rent the effort of the team, but great leaders earn the commitment of heads and hearts. Lead with purpose.

Day 277

What did you say you were going to do this week for your team? Did you do it? What about the goals and vision you laid out at the beginning of the year - have you followed through on your part of the commitment? Or are you, like I have a tendency to be, someone who shares an inspiring vision and then doesn't hold up your end of the bargain? It's not intentional or purposeful, it just happens. Life gets in the way, another exciting things comes along and your attention goes elsewhere. Or maybe you were inspired by the idea at the moment and had to share it, but didn't communicate clearly that you weren't committed.

We can give speeches and lay out grand visions and share how we're going to help our team achieve new heights. But we destroy our influence and credibility if our presence ends there. Eventually others catch on to our tendencies. Eventually they stop buying in. Eventually they realize that though we mean well, we won't act.

Lots of folks can talk about what they hope to do or the culture they hope to create. Leaders actually do the work. Action creates change. Be known for your actions.

Day 278

Love your team. Of course, but how did you do that yesterday? How will you show it today?

Value the contribution each person brings. That's a no-brainer, but do all of them know you value what they bring to the table? Even the person who is hard to talk to sometimes?

Communicate, communicate, communicate. We all know that, but how many things did you fail to mention yesterday because you assumed your teammates already knew it (when of course they didn't)?

What seems simple and obvious isn't always easy. Show up today with purpose. Empower, communicate and lead intentionally.

Day 279

Nobody has your unique gifts and experiences. Even though some people may have the same personality wiring as you, they've not lived your life. They've not seen what you have seen, done what you have done, learned what you have learned. When we see others who are successful (whatever "successful" may mean), we often want to mimic them. "It worked for them so it will work for me." But you aren't them and they aren't you.

Rather than mimicking someone, take what he does well and apply it to your own strengths and weaknesses. This, of course, starts with knowing your own strengths and weaknesses. Great leadership is rooted in self-awareness.

You can copy someone else's leadership style or you can develop and be confident in your own. We need your best you. Lead with authenticity.

Day 280

An overpowering leader builds a compliant team. A team of people that shows up because they have to, that does the work because they are paid to. Many times, the team operates under a spirit of fear, just waiting for the leader to blow up. There may be short term wins because the work is getting done, but the long-term picture looks unproductive and unattractive.

An empowering leader builds a committed team. A team that works toward a shared vision. A team who knows the leader is for each of them, which results in them wanting to do great work. They believe their work matters, that it is more than a paycheck. A committed team creates sustainable success.

Compliant teams are overpowered, committed teams are empowered. The culture of your team is a result of your leadership. Lead intentionally.

Day 281

Standing just behind the shortstop during my oldest son's baseball game, I looked around at the players. Some were dialed in, some were talking to each other, some were playing in the dirt, some were dancing. A runner was on first base, and the head coach yelled out, "The play is at either second or first!" The play is at either second or first! Get ready! Watch the batter!" Immediately, the eyes of each player went to the batter. You could almost see the thought go through their brains, "Oh, right. Baseball. That's what I'm here for. I might need to catch the ball. And throw it. To first base. Or second. The play is at either second or first."

Consistently throughout the game, the coach reminded them of where they were going and what they were doing. Fighting through heat, fatigue and just the general distractions of 7-year-olds, he had to be the voice they heard and responded to.

Leadership, I think is the same way. Our teams will fight through down seasons, through distractions, through too many things begging for their attention. They'll forget where we are and where we're going. If we don't speak up, the moment will pass them by and we'll be playing catch-up.

Leaders are a guiding voice, consistently reminding the team of where we're going and what we're doing. In the midst of distractions, leaders bring clarity.

Day 282

You have an idea. It's going to be amazing and change the world and your team is going to be on board because it's just that incredible. Reality check: everyone has ideas. Everyone has a vision. Those who make the most impact are those who know how to bring that vision to life. Because a vision without a plan isn't really a vision.

Without the how, you have the blind leading the blind. As an idea guy, I'm speaking from experience. I have a vision but don't more often than not I don't have the legs to get us there.

Eventually your team will realize you don't know how to get where you want to go and you'll destroy your influence and credibility. Take time to process your vision. What's step one? Two? 10? Is there someone on your team who can help you bring clarity to it?

Don't just share the vision — show the plan. The why doesn't matter or happen without the how.

Day 283

We've been talking about taking a family vacation to Great Wolf Lodge in Dallas. If we head out from Oklahoma City and go north on I-35, we'll never get there. No matter how much we want to go to Dallas, no matter how good our intentions are, we'll end up in Wichita or Kansas City or somewhere in between. To go to Dallas, we have to go the right direction. We can't hope we end up there; we have to take the necessary action.

The same is true for our lives and for our teams. What we want doesn't matter if we don't take steps toward it. We can't hope for less drama while we gossip about others. We can't hope for better communication and never be clear about expectations. We can't hope for healthy culture while consistently undermining our efforts.

Do you know what you want for you and your team this week and, more importantly, do you know how to get there? Direction, not intention, determines your destination.

Day 284

We all have seasons that bring stress. Seasons where we have too many late nights at the office, too many meals eaten at our desk rather than with friends and family, where we are stuck in a mode we can't change. If we're intentional, we can schedule some rest during those times so we don't reach burnout.

The issue comes when that season turns into a climate. That's when an addiction to work becomes a way of life, when those you value get pushed to the side, when you undermine your influence in every circle. It's when we ultimately crash.

Do you know your tendencies to prevent this from happening? Do you know the signs that you're on the precipice of an unhealthy life? Do those around you know them, so they can help keep you accountable and be a system of support and challenge? If we know our tendencies we can choose new actions. We can go left instead of right. We can choose presence rather than productivity. We can choose to rest rather than get one more hour of work done.

If we don't make rest a priority, our body - as well as our family and friends - will force the issue.

Don't let a season of busyness and stress turn into a climate that results in burnout and damaged influence. We need work but we also need relationship and rest.

Day 285

Which do you value more on your team, character or talent? Both are needed but most leaders focus on talent. "I'll hire talented people, they'll do their job and I won't have to worry about it." Accidental leadership at its finest (or worst). You end up with a team of talented people who don't get along, don't know why and, the worst part, they don't care. It's a talented but disconnected group. Even wins, in this environment, can feel like losses.

Stress will reveal deep character issues that become unbearable and lead to hard changes. This is why most organizations get their hiring process wrong. They hire for talent but fire for character.

Talent will win in the short-term but lack of character eventually catches up and destroys a team.

Leaders worth following value character first, then develop talent.

Day 286

You notice something and don't speak up, assuming everyone else notices it as well. You see an obvious piece of the puzzle, of the goal your team is striving for, yet say nothing because you think the team understands it. "Of course they get it. How could they not?"

You have a unique set of skills, a unique perspective. You see things nobody else does. If you don't say something, you are setting the team up for frustration and bitterness. (by the way, the same is true for everyone on the team. Empower others to speak up as well.)

What is obvious to you is most likely not obvious to those around you. If you won't speak up, who will? Your words may be the catalyst for a needed change.

Day 287

What gets in the way of you making the right decision for the team? What stops you from doing what is necessary, choosing instead to abdicate? What causes you to gossip and/or get passive aggressive, rather than having the direct conversation that is needed?

The battle for a leader is not good vs. evil, it is pride vs humility. Pride makes us feel like we have something to prove, it causes us to overprotect, it causes us to hide. Pride turns our leadership inward. We become for ourselves rather than for others.

Prideful leaders give in — to fear, insecurity and self-preservation. Humble, secure, confident leaders have nothing to lose, nothing to prove, nothing to hide.

Show up for the best of those you lead.

Day 288

Is your team all about work or is there time and opportunity to know each other, to become more than just co-workers? Is that "work only" mindset coming from you? Leaders set the tone.

If we don't connect with the people on our team, we value them only for their work. We don't know their motivations and aspirations, we don't know when they need picked up (or how to pick them up). We see them as a salesperson, graphic designer, HR manager or intern, rather than a person with a story.

If we know those around us we not only value them but know how to show them they are valued. When things get down we're able to say, "I've got your back. Deal with what you need to deal with, we're here for you." We're able to fight for their highest good because we want it for them. We know them as Mitchell, Tonya, Andre.

The work matters but not as much as the people. A connected team of talented people is capable of greatness.

People on disconnected teams tend to work for themselves rather than the good of the team. Value both presence and productivity. Leaders define culture.

Day 289

When you view leadership as a position or title, you stunt the growth of those you lead. Leadership becomes a promotion to be earned, a ladder to climb, a competition to win. There will always be people left out, who feel unqualified and undervalued. It's a quick way to have a team of people who aren't engaged, who show up out of obligation.

When you view leadership as a way of life, you realize everyone you lead is capable of being a leader. Everyone becomes worth investing in, everyone becomes valuable, everyone has a place at the table regardless of title.

Everyone is capable of being a leader worth following - it is not a title on an org chart. A team of leaders is better than a team of employees.

Day 290

It's easy to show up today and work through your to-do list, exchange minor pleasantries with those you lead and those around you, head home at the end of the day and then repeat it again tomorrow and the next day. It's easy to keep every conversation surface level, not truly getting to know your team. It's easy to focus purely on the desired outcomes of the work. This is what the world expects. This is what "leadership" has looked like for most of our lives.

A friend recently noted how it feels like the idea of what a leader is, or should be, is being completely transformed at this moment in history. He said that he's always felt like he needed to be rigid, logical, tactical. Almost militaristic. "Now I'm realizing just how terrible of a leader I would be if I lived into that." Don't care how people feel about you and don't care how people feel in general — just get the job done and win. This leadership style over time leads to fear, manipulation and burnout. It silences the voice of everyone around them. It's overpowering.

The reality of leadership today is that you must know and invest in your people. Know what drives and motivates them. Know and speak their language. Know their stories and how they fit uniquely into the story of the team. You have to not only challenge them, but support them. If you don't, you'll undermine your influence as a leader. They may trust your credibility and competency, but they won't trust your character.

When you truly know those you lead, you can value their perspective and know how to fight for their highest good. Don't overpower them, empower them.

Day 291

"What is best for me?" That's the question most of us ask when faced with a decision. We look for the choice that helps us win, the option that gets us ahead. It's not inherently a bad question but for a leader, it takes those you lead out of the equation.

A better question is, "What is best for those around me?" What decision is the right move for your team? What option is a win for your family? Think of others before you make a decision for yourself. It may seem counterintuitive, but being a leader worth following typically is.

What is best for you is not always what is best for those you lead. Don't put your agenda ahead of the vision.

Day 292

Pride is destructive for a leader. I say this as a person who struggles with pride. If I'm not intentional, I tend to make my life and my leadership all about me. It's ugly. It's one thing to say you're prideful, it's another to know how that impacts others. That's why I always come back to the question for leaders, "Do you know what it's like to be on the other side of you?"

I don't know that I've solved the pride issue but it's certainly become less of an issue for me. How? Focusing on others. In my work, in my life, in my relationships, my goal has to be to serve, empower and better those I'm with. When doing social media sessions with athletes and administrators, my goal isn't to be the greatest speaker; my goal is to help them believe they have a story worth telling and empower them to tell it. When working with teams and leaders, I'm not trying to be the next great leadership guru. I simply want to help people realize they are capable of being leaders worth following who can change their world for the better.

I get to make them the heroes. I just show up and fight for their highest good. Pride would limit and undermine all of those efforts.

Lay down your agenda and fight for the highest good of those you lead. When you lead to serve others, pride doesn't have room to operate.

Day 293

Today is not all about you. If leadership is influence and influence is power, power is the capacity to influence. True power is given to you by others. Don't try to take it. Influence is a privilege. To get it you must be for others, not yourself. Intent matters.

You may lose personally in the short-term when you put others before yourself, but you will always win in the long run. Be for others today.

Day 294

Are you making decisions based on what gets people closer to the vision, or are you making decisions to protect yourself? When you find your identity in your work and in your role/title, you do whatever you can to keep it. You put yourself before others; you put your goals above those of the team. Leaders worth following lead not for themselves, but for their teams.

Your ambition matters but cannot come at the expense of those around you. You achieve your best when you help others pursue and become their best.

Day 295

When was the last time you were challenged? For many of you, you probably took it as criticism. It wounded you and threw you off for the rest of the day. It resulted in a distance between you and those who brought challenge. "How could they be so direct, so hurtful, so negative?"

What if they weren't being personal? What if they weren't being hurtful? Maybe they could have delivered their challenge more appropriately, but what if their hearts were in the right place?

In a recent session with a team where we focused on self-awareness, a woman came up at the end with tears forming in her eyes and said, "Thank you so much for this. My teammates are always telling me to be nicer and I think I am being nice. Now they can see where I'm coming from. That I truly love them and want what is best for us. I'm just wired differently and that truth comes out in a different way. And I also have a better understanding of how they're receiving my words. I get how they could think I was being rude. I feel like the weight of the world was just lifted off my shoulders. This changes everything."

When we know what it's like on the other side of us and we trust the intent of those around us, everything changes. Drama decreases, communication increases, teams and relationships thrive.

To take things personally is a choice. The person bringing you challenge may be fighting for your highest good. Trust their intent.

Day 296

You don't have all the answers. You can't fix every problem. You won't succeed at every project. You can't motivate every employee. You can't please every teammate, donor, media member, fan. You can't do it all.

Don't feel defeated by that. Release yourself from the pressure of being everything to everyone. Find freedom in that truth.

Your attitude as you walk into the office sets the tone for the week, both for you and for those you lead. Empty your mind of the negativity that comes from worrying about what you can't do, and fill it with enthusiasm for the opportunities ahead.

Day 297

In old school martial arts, their masters are not judged by their skills. Instead, they are judged by the skills of their students. Their leadership is not an inward thing, focused only on self-improvement; it is about the development of others.

How are those around you better for having you as a leader? *Are* they better? Would they say your leadership is about you or do they know it is for them? Do they believe they're capable of more than they were this time last year because you encourage and empower them, or do they believe they are just another piece in the machine? Do they know you're fighting for their highest possible good, day in and day out?

Leadership is about developing greatness in others. Leaders worth following build leaders worth following.

Day 298

Sitting with a friend who is a senior leader in the corporate world but has also been a coach, I asked him about his approach to leadership. Whether he's coaching a player, a team, an employee or his kids, his question to them is, "What does a win look like for you today?"

I thought it was a simple but profound question. It reminds me of golf, a game I love but also find incredibly frustrating. All it takes, though, is one great swing to get me excited to come back for another round. One swing out of 80 (or 90 or 100 - depending on the current status of your golf game). One good shot and that voice inside your head says, "You can do this! Keep going!"

If we don't define a daily win - and celebrate it - we will never move forward. Our energy drains and our focus is gone. We forget where we're going and eventually just show up because we have to.

In the midst of the daily grind, it's easy to lose sight of our why. What does a win look like for you today? What about for your team? Define it, celebrate it, build on it.

Day 299

In a recent interview, Amazon CEO Jeff Bezos was reflecting on the failed Amazon Fire Phone. His quote on the failure resonated with me. "If you think that's a big failure, we're working on much bigger failures now. And I'm not kidding. And some of them are going to make the Fire Phone look like a tiny little blip." Amazon is, without question, one of the most successful organizations on the planet. How did it get there? Hundreds (probably millions) of failures that led to a small number of wins.

This is a crucial mindset for a leader. Too often we're paralyzed by the worst possible outcome of what will happen if our idea fails. An outcome that, even if we do fail, isn't likely. Odds are low that we get fired, get demoted, lose our family, lose our house, lose our respect/reputation, etc. Approached with the right mindset (and humility), a failure gets us closer to a win. A failure brings clarity to the path forward.

Don't be afraid of failure. Failure means you took a step forward, you said the status quo isn't good enough, you went for a better version of tomorrow. Lean in.

Day 300

Leadership is less about the head and more about the heart. You can read a book and pass that information on to your team but will it change anyone? Did it really change you? There's a time for information, but true influence comes through transformation. Something that stirs you, something that leaves you different than before. It comes from thinking about your team as more than people to manage, but as heroes to empower. That kind of impact and influence ripples through every area of their lives.

Informed leaders can change minds. Transformed leaders change lives. Envision the best possible future for your team and go for it this week.

Day 301

We spend most of our life fighting for ourselves. We go to school, we work on our craft, we we seek out the right job and work to get the right promotion. None of this is inherently bad. We live in a culture that praises achievers, so we set our sights on a goal that takes us to the next level and we set out to achieve it. At the end we look back and say, "This is what I have achieved, this is what I have produced."

The problem is that this is a very inward focus. It becomes all about my career, my needs, my brand. The greatest leaders are those who realize their lives should be about others. How can you help those you lead take the next step? How can you help them become great? How can you fight for their highest good so that they can then go fight for the highest good of others? Leaders worth following build leaders worth following who build leaders worth following.

A life focused on ourselves begins and ends with us. A life focused on others reaches generations. Leaders worth following are for others, today and every day.

Day 302

After a break of six weeks due to travel and fighting off a cold, I went back out for a run. I felt like I was good enough to get out and I was desperately in need of some recharge. So I laced up and off I went.

Less than a mile in, I thought I was going to die. My legs felt great but I couldn't breathe. I was coughing, searching for breath, struggling to get any sort of rhythm. In a three-mile-run I ended up stopping five times just to try to get my breath. And it wasn't due to speed - I was running just off my normal pace, trying to not overdo it my first day back.

It was incredibly frustrating. My legs were good but my lungs wouldn't let me.

Our teams and organizations are the same way. We have strong, talented individuals but we have a culture that isn't healthy. And no matter how talented our people are, talent in a bad culture has limits. Talent gets undermined by drama, gossip, lack of clarity and unclear communication. We may eventually achieve the desired goal but at what cost? The end result is not always what matters.

Talent matters, but culture is the oxygen of your team. A healthy culture breathes life into everything you do. A toxic culture suffocates. Create culture intentionally.

Day 303

We spend an awful lot of time talking about issues or ideas. We have the perfect solution for this, or the right way to do that. Unfortunately, we spend more time talking than doing. The same issues come up in meeting after meeting. The same problems keep popping up. As leaders, we often think we've done our job simply by pointing out a problem. Rather than sit back and direct, leaders must go first. We must set the tone. Identifying a problem is only half the battle. Take action.

Leaders don't just talk about an issue. They are compelled to act. Take the first step and your team will follow. Be more than your words.

Day 304

How do you you respond when people question your ideas? Do you get defensive and immediately start arguing? Do you shut them down and move on with the discussion? Do you go into a "you're either for me or against me" mindset? Or do you see it as an opportunity to refine your ideas?

Some of the people on your team will ask questions to make sure you're utilizing time and resources in the best possible way, to make sure you actually have a plan. Others will ask questions to make sure you've thought of the impact on the people. All will help you see your idea and vision in a new, clearer way and illuminate the best way forward. That is, if you let them. If you embrace their questions, if you give them permission to speak up.

Insecure leaders can't be questioned. Secure leaders welcome those who bring clarity to the vision.

Day 305

Your team puts on its best face and appears to do the best work when you're in the room but what happens when you leave? You're told everything is "fine" but as soon as you're gone, the truth comes out. Frustration, bitterness, lack of trust. You can blame the team for this, or you can own your role in the situation. How has your leadership contributed to this reality?

Leadership is reflected in how your team works when you're not present. Create a culture where people want to consistently bring their best.

Day 306

Two kinds of leaders we consistently run into: those who appear to overvalue what they bring to the table and those who undervalue what they bring to the table. Those who overvalue their contribution tend to speak up out of insecurity. Their loudness is typically masking the reality that they don't want to be found out as a fraud. So they undervalue their strengths but "overcome" it by appearing to overvalue them. The walls of self-preservation have to come down in order for them to realize their full potential.

On the flip side, those who undervalue their contribution tend to operate in silence. They don't want to be seen because they feel like a fraud. It could be that they've been run over by a dominating leader or they've just never fully known their voice and their value. They need support, encouragement, empowerment.

Leaders worth following know their strengths and their weaknesses. They value their contribution as well as those who complement them. Lead securely, confidently, humbly.

Day 307

You can talk down to your team, strike fear into people, show them you're the boss. You can point out every weakness and criticize every failure. You can make them fall in line, submitting to your every command. And you just might hit all of your goals along the way. You can claim "success" and the metrics on financial statements would agree with you. But is that really success?

That kind of environment is surprisingly normal (or maybe that's not surprising to you at all because you're living it - hopefully you're not leading it). In that situation, you've become a leader people have to follow. They do what they are told, they follow the rules, they complete the task.

Empower, don't overpower. Liberate, don't dominate. Build up, don't tear down.

Success isn't always defined by wins and losses. Success comes from the culture created along the journey. Be a leader people want to follow.

Day 308

Today, ask more questions and give less answers. Offer more support and prescribe fewer solutions. Listen more than you talk. Cheer on more than you direct. Encourage more than you criticize.

Be intentionally about your team today. The work matters, but the people always come first.

Day 309

How do we keep our employees happy? Pay them or give them more benefits? Money is not the motivator most believe it to be. Money and perks are actually an easy out. "Look what we did for you." It doesn't require you to actually know or engage with your people. You just throw a meeting announcing the "exciting news" that every employee now gets free gym membership and pat yourself on the back for a job well done. Of course, next year it'll be a different perk, and the cycle continues.

The truth? Your team wants and needs to feel known, valued, connected. People want to know you're for them. This requires you to be intentional, to truly know each person on your team, to speak their language. Your knowledge and skills aren't enough. The company perks aren't enough. They need to know you care.

People don't want to be managed, they want to be led. They need leadership that connects with them, values them, knows them. An empowered team is an unstoppable team.

Day 310

Know yourself to lead yourself.

Becoming a leader worth following.

Know your team to lead your team.

Leaders define culture.

Lead intentionally, not accidentally.

Leaders set the tone.

Fight for the highest possible good of those you lead.

Culture trumps strategy.

Be for your team.

You'll notice these phrases, among others, are often repeated in this book. They are phrases we use during our sessions with teams and leaders. Hang around the office or listen in on one of our group calls and you'll hear them as well. Many of them are also spoken daily in my house. Why? Because we're human and we forget things.

If we're not reminded of what we're doing, where we're going, whom we're trying to become and why, we'll forget. We easily get distracted and consumed with our daily tasks and lose sight of the bigger picture. It's why people often give up on goals and resolutions. As life gets in the way, they stop reminding themselves of their goals. It's often not that they consciously give up, they just lose focus.

Ask those on your team if they know what they're working toward and why. If they don't know the answer, you're not communicating vision often enough (and/or clearly enough). A common vocabulary establishes a leadership language that helps to create an intentional culture.

Vision leaks. As leaders, it's on us to clearly and consistently communicate a compelling vision. Lead intentionally.

Day 311

What dreams do you have for yourself? What goals, ambitions, pursuits drive you? When you envision your best future, what does it look like?

Do you dream those same things for those you lead or are you using them to achieve your dream?

Leaders worth following desire for others what they desire for themselves. Fight for the highest possible good of those you lead.

Day 312

When drama hits on your team, what do you do? When everyone is negative, fighting for himself rather than for each other, how do you respond? Do you give into the culture of negativity and add to the drama? It's certainly the easy thing to do. "What good does it do if I'm the one positive person around here? What's really going to change if I keep showing up with purpose?"

When I was in the corporate world, I gave in to the drama. I joined the gossiping and negativity. I took the easy way out. And I completely undermined my influence. Years later, I ended up going back to one leader in particular and apologizing for my immaturity. For being a follower rather than a leader. For accepting what was rather than changing it.

The culture won't change if you don't change it. It isn't always easy. You have to intentionally choose your path and your mindset each day. Your team will follow your lead.

Day 313

Becoming a leader worth following isn't easy. Because we're human and imperfect, it's not something we can ever really attain. It's a journey of choices, of self-awareness, of intent. The journey is difficult but worth it.

The reality is that many want to be great leaders but few want to do the work. Of the few who do take the first steps, many give up because of the resistance they face. They try to implement what they've learned and their teams just give them blank stares.

A leader I was coaching mentioned that as she started saying and doing this differently, her team would look at her like, "Who are you? What's happening?" Over time, though, they realized that she was serious. That she was different and that, while she certainly would still make mistakes, her mindset had changed. It would've been easy for her to give up, to say this doesn't work, to go back to her old ways. But she stuck with it and it paid off.

The same is true with your team. Dig in, stay strong, do the hard work, don't give up. Who you are becoming and who you are empowering others to become is worth the difficult days.

Your team doesn't know that the leader you were is not the leader you're becoming. People honor consistency. Keep showing up.

Day 314

Are you shaping culture or are you being shaped by culture?

To be shaped by culture is to be distracted by every new thing, to be inconsistent, to not speak up, to chase trends. It's a sign that you've lost your why. It is accidental leadership.

To shape culture is to be intentional, to know where you are going and why, to be clear in what is expected and what is allowed, to understand when "no" is necessary.

Leaders who are shaped by culture are abdicating their responsibility. Leaders who shape culture are transforming the world around them. Lead intentionally.

Day 315

I was a huge fan of the show *Ace of Cakes* on the Food Network, and am as much of a fan of the newer version called *Cake Masters*. The shows follow Chef Duff Goldman and his team of cake makers - though "master" is definitely a more fitting term. The team creates the most creative, off the wall, "can this be real?" cakes for their clients. From cakes shaped like a guitar that you can actually play, to action figures that move and fight. If it's beyond what you can think, they can do it.

While I'm fan of the creativity, I'm also consumed by their team dynamics. Duff is a boisterous, larger than life personality. He's a former rock musician who is full of big ideas, executes on them and has fun while doing it. And, for the camera's view, he's an incredible leader. He's put together a team of people with incredibly unique talents and personalities who are constantly performing under extreme stress. Many of these cakes require long days and late nights and they often work right up to the moment they have to carefully load it in the van for delivery.

Duff challenges his team to pull off cakes they don't think are possible, yet balances that with an incredible amount of encouragement, support and praise. He knows his crew is made up of rock stars and, rather than just thinking it, he makes sure to tell them. It's a demanding job yet the turnover is minimal. The team continues to show up, continues to have a great attitude, continues to execute. Even tense moments (healthy teams debate) are handled respectfully.

So why does it work? Why are they willing to go to such extreme lengths to make cakes? First, they know Duff is for them. He's hard, he can be obnoxious, but he loves them and they know it. They don't have to follow him, they want to. Second, they are empowered to be their best. Their voices and talents aren't suppressed. All of them have roles to play and they know know those roles (and their skills and opinions) are valued. Every voice matters, everyone gets to play. Third, they buy into the mission. They believe in the work and know that the next client could truly be "their next greatest adventure."

When your team members know you are for them, knows they matter and fully believes in the mission, anything is possible. Leaders set the tone.

Day 316

The truth? I wake up every day with doubt. Am I good enough? Can I do this? Can I build to companies? Can I make a difference? Can I really help student-athletes, coaches, administrators and athletics departments tell their stories online? Can I really help transform the leadership culture in college athletics? It's enough to cripple a person.

Except it doesn't. I get up and go to work. I make calls, schedule meetings, travel the country to speak and to serve leaders to empower them to change their world for the better. I show up. It isn't always easy, and the doubt is always there, but I show up.

Doubt doesn't win. Fear doesn't win. The status quo doesn't win.

Doubt isn't a sign of weakness for a leader. Inaction is. Show up today and take a step forward.

Day 317

Everyone around you is a leader. That shouldn't threaten you; that should excite you. You want a team of leaders. The question is what kind of leaders surround you? Leaders who are humble, secure and confident or leaders who are insecure, paranoid and selfish? Is your organization full of people who are for themselves or for others?

The world doesn't need more leaders, it needs better leaders. We need leaders worth following, leaders worth multiplying. It starts with you.

Day 318

Culture is how the receptionist answers the phone and welcomes guests when they arrive. Culture is how you speak to people in meetings. Culture is how people are allowed to work, discuss, debate, create. Culture is how you handle stressful situations and how you handle success. Culture is shown in how you view and treat people, from the janitor to your peers to your boss. Culture dictates how you hire and how you fire. Culture shapes the vision for tomorrow and the work done today to get there.

Culture infiltrates every aspect of an organization, intentionally or accidentally. Don't hope for it, create it.

Day 319

Habits are born out of choices. Choices that, over time, become second nature. Choices that change who we were into who we will be.

Today's habit becomes tomorrow's reality. If we want new results, we must make new choices.

Leadership is a habit. A result of making the choice today to be for people, to be better than yesterday. Then making that decision tomorrow, and the next day, and the next.

Day 320

What do you believe makes a great leader? What do you think makes a great team? Are these things thoughts in your head or do they actually shape the way you lead?

What we think matters, but it must shape what we do and what we don't do.

Many people believe things about about leadership. Leaders live out their beliefs.

Day 321

You can motivate your team today but when will that wear off? Weeks? Months? You can offer incentives, but those will wear off as well. Culture, on the other hand, sticks. It values every voice and empowers everyone to bring the best, every day. It's a way of life. It invites everyone to participate. It gets at the heart of the issue, of the team, of the organization.

Leaders worth following don't rely on gimmicks or motivational tactics. They realize the only way to create long term change is to invest in culture.

Day 322

Culture will make your team members excited to come to work each day or it will make them show up because they have to show up. Culture will make people stick around when things get tough or it will be the thing that drives them away. Culture is what will attract others to your department or it will be what keeps your candidate pool low.

Culture is what people talk about when they discuss your program.

Culture is the operating system of your organization. It's happening, with or without you. Leaders set the tone. Create culture intentionally.

Day 323

Together. A simple but powerful word reminding us, as leaders, that we are not the answer. Not everything falls on us. The team and organization should not rely on you. If you leave and everything falls apart, you've not done your job. Leadership isn't about one person, it's about the whole.

Leaders are at their best when they use their influence to help those they lead become their best. When they empower rather control. Everyone moving forward, together.

Day 324

Today will have its difficulties and frustrations.

Your team will misunderstand you. Your budget may be cut by 10%. Another department may hire one of your all-stars. A player may leave.

You may be in the midst of a great season when one of these things happens. It may feel like a shock to the system. "We were just finding our groove. Where did this come from?"

You can complain or you can learn and lead. A road without obstacles is a road that will do you no good.

Leaders can't get comfortable. It's dangerous. Growth won't come without uncomfortable moments. Lean in and fight through it.

Day 325

Do you want the best out of your people? Do you want them to come to work excited, energized, committed to do their best? Or do you want people to show up because it's a paycheck, to go through the motions each day because it's what they are supposed to do?

The answer is obvious. We all want our teams to show up with excitement, passion and purpose. The real question is what are you doing to make that the reality?

What matters to people, in terms of work happiness, is feeling like they are doing work that matters, feeling like they are valued and heard, feeling like they are more than a line on the budget. Culture matters.

When you know and value those on your team, they feel empowered to bring their best each day.

Day 326

You are not the hero for your team. When you think you're the hero, you make your leadership, your influence and your work about you. Leaders worth following are for others.

The reality is that most people wake up believing they are the hero. What they are looking for is a guide. Someone to help them. When you make your leadership about others, you get to be the guide. Then when they're ready, those you lead will become the guides for others. Leaders worth following build leaders worth following.

Leaders act as the guide for their team, not the hero. They participate in the transformation of those they lead, helping them become somebody better than they used to be.

Day 327

At the heart of most frustration, most bitterness, most drama, most issues on a team is unclear communication. Sometimes it is lack of communication, but most often it is unclear communication. You may feel like you've communicated to your team, but not everyone heard you. "Well, I said it so I don't know what the issue is. There's only so many ways I can say it." Exactly. There are more ways to say it and you have to know which way will connect with each person on your team. Getting up and sharing a message may only land correctly with 20% of your team. Everyone else was in the room and they heard you, but they didn't *hear* you.

As the leader, it's on you to communicate the right way with each person. Your messaging and style should change for each person on your team. Not to manipulate them, but to connect with them. If you can't speak their language, you can't lead them.

Day 328

Work is work, but it doesn't have to be a burden. When you reflect on the process after achieving a goal, hitting a milestone, getting the championship, you want your team to not only be proud of the goal, but also to have enjoyed the grind. If you look back with disdain, what motivation is there to do it again other than you have to? Your team grows apart, each person working only for the sake of working.

When you look back and are able to laugh about the good and bad times from start to finish, you want to dust yourself off and get back at it. Your team members have become closer, knows they are there for each other, and knows each person is valued and has a role. That is something worth celebrating. That is a culture worth multiplying.

Winning without having fun isn't winning. Success without joy isn't success.

Don't create a culture where people produce out of fear and obligation. Success is difficult but should be enjoyed. Be a team, not a department.

Day 329

Leaders are dreamers. Leaders are visionaries. Leaders are innovators. Leaders pay attention to the details. Leaders embrace what's needed now. Leaders are loud. Leaders are reserved. Leaders are crazy passionate. Leaders don't give into their emotions.

Read enough books and you'll hear a "leader" described every way imaginable, with each description seemingly contradicting another. The reality is that leaders come in all shapes and sizes, all personality types and backgrounds.

Leaders operate out of their strengths, are self-aware enough to know their weaknesses and surround themselves with people who complement them.

Day 330

"I know we've been focused on growth, but I think now we should really worry about retaining customers. That's what matters." Then next month, it'll be brand awareness and the next month it'll be average revenue per customer and the next month something else.

"Most of our efforts have gone to this platform, and last quarter it was that platform, then before that it was a different one, but let's worry about this hot thing for now." Of course that will change in a few weeks when a new platform comes out.

There are times when we need to shift our focus and change direction, but if this is your norm for you, you are undermining your influence. Every month or quarter you bring something to your team that is the latest and greatest and is going to change everything. Folks have seen the dog-and-pony show enough to know that it won't last, that next month it'll be something new. They put on their fake smiles, take the book and add it to the stack of others that haven't been read or implemented.

Inconsistent leaders undermine their influence and will eventually be tuned out by their team. They'll follow you, but only because they have to.

Day 331

"I'm not good enough," is a lie too many leaders (and too many of the people you lead) believe. It's a lie that paralyzes them. It causes their decisions and actions to be based out of fear and self-preservation.

Are you the leader you want to be? Of course not...yet. None of us are. And that's OK. It's certainly no reason to doubt yourself.

Despite the gap between who you are and who you are becoming, believe that today you are enough. Today, you are better than yesterday.

Day 332

I was holding our youngest son one day when he was about eight weeks old, and he started to get fussy. I randomly decided to laugh as hard as I could. In the midst of his fussiness, he started smiling. A giggle or two even came out. My other boys were in the room and they started laughing. Joy, even in the midst of frustration, is contagious.

You will have stress today. Deadlines will be missed, goals won't be hit, hard conversations will take place, people will disappoint. To ignore that reality is irresponsible but you have a choice in how you respond.

To let your circumstances control you is to be an inconsistent, emotional leader. In the midst of the chaos and stress of the day, choose to lead and respond with joy.

Day 333

The world is full of critics who don't take action. "You should have done this." "I would have done it this way." "It will never work that way." They read all of the books and attend every conference yet, for all they supposedly know, they never get off the sideline. Rather than using their knowledge and preparation to make a difference, they sit back and point out the problems. They take the easy way out. The way that requires no risk and results in no growth or influence.

Leaders don't sit on the sideline and criticize. They join in the battle and help find a solution.

Day 334

"No, we don't have the resources."

"Sorry, we don't have time for that."

"Wish we could but our budget won't allow it."

How many times each day do you tell your team no?

What would change if you said yes?

When all our people hear is "no" they stop showing up with purpose. They stop thinking about how to make things better and instead just want to get the job done. And, sure, things are getting done but nothing is getting better. Nobody wants to be a part of a team like that and, if we're honest, nobody wants to lead a team like that.

Saying "yes" to our people gives them energy. It gives them permission to create. They get to think of what could be, then make it reality.

"I like it, but here's our budget. Get creative and let me know what you come up with." It's saying, "I'm with you, I'm for you, we probably can't do all of it but let's go for it and see what we can do." 80% of a new idea is better than the status quo.

That's how your team grows. That's how you get better. That's how you move forward and adapt and succeed. That's how you get a committed team.

Tomorrow won't be better than today if we always say "no" to our team. Saying "yes" creates a culture of innovation and commitment.

Day 335

When you seek power, there will always be more to get. When you seek control, there will never be enough. When you seek protection, there will always be more perceived threats. These are the concerns of insecure leaders.

Secure leaders, leaders worth following, don't pursue power, control or protection. They seek out opportunities to empower.

Day 336

The words we use as leaders matter. When you're for others, your words reflect that. It's not about me, it's about us. The successes are ours, not mine. In the same way, when you are for yourself your team can feel it through the words you speak. People hear you say they screwed up when things go wrong but that you did a great job when goals are hit. They'll follow you because they have to, not because they want to.

The language of a leader reflects his intentions. Let your words show your team that you are for everyone's highest good.

Day 337

Every decision is a crossroads, every conversation an opportunity. We are tempted by culture, by the shiny new thing, by what is trendy. Our attention is divided and every morning there is something "new and better" pulling us in. It's easy to give in, to go with the crowd.

Sift through the noise, step back and ask, "What is the wise and right thing to do?" Popular is easy — wise is needed.

What is right and needed is not necessarily what is popular. Leaders don't give in to culture. Leaders create culture.

Day 338

Regardless of what your title is, you are responsible for the culture on your team. You have a say in what behavior and actions are allowed. If someone is toxic, you have to take ownership to make it right. If people are doing great work without being noticed, it's your job to make sure they are celebrated. We are responsible for the culture around us.

We become leaders the moment we decide we're responsible for the culture of our team. Take ownership, take action.

Day 339

A great leader is intentional about being surrounded by other great leaders. That doesn't always mean hiring great leaders. Most times it simply means investing in those they lead. The best leaders use their wisdom, position and influence to apprentice those they lead to become impactful leaders. They don't view others as a threat, they view them as potential leaders who can add value to the team and make the team great.

Want to know if a leader is worth following? Look at those they lead. Leaders worth following build teams of leaders worth following.

Day 340

You gave a rousing speech to your team a year ago, then retreated into your office for the next month. You sent an inspiring email six months later, then proceeded to be moody and let the events of the day dictate your emotions for the next few weeks. You found a motivating video on YouTube, sent it to your team with a note encouraging your team to charge the hill, then you changed course a week later. You read a leadership book that "really moved you" and handed out copies to your team, only to never implement any of the ideas in the book.

We don't show up every so often, say something noteworthy and check off our leadership to-do list for the quarter. Leadership is who we are and what we do every day.

Day 341

Those around you have hopes and dreams, fears and insecurities. They've been burned by leaders and they've had amazing mentors. Some have incredible ideas about the future of your team and are afraid to speak up, wondering if they are "important" enough to do so. Others spout off ideas seemingly without thinking but if you give them a minute, they'll figure out what they really believe. There are those who have failed and those who will fail. There are those who want nothing more than to know they matter. Your team is full of people who are worth knowing.

People. At the end of the day, leaders are in the people business. The more we take the time to know and invest in our people, the better we can lead them and the more unstoppable our team can be.

Day 342

Think back over the course of your life. Think about people who were influential, who played a significant role. It could be something as simple as a conversation or words of wisdom, or someone who walked alongside you for a season as a mentor. Parents, grandparents, coaches, teachers, professors, bosses, friends and more. Many times as leaders we have a tendency to sit back and say, "Look at what I've built, at what I've earned." When we have that type of mindset, we spend our days trying to protect "what we've built."

While our hard work certainly plays a role in our success, the reality is that our success is the result of the time and energy that others poured into us. Are you doing that for those around you? Are you the kind of leader they will look back on as playing a key role in their success?

We are not entitled to our position or influence. When we view them as gifts, we realize our role is to use them for the good of others.

Day 343

"If only they thought about things the way I do. If I could just get them to do it my way." Those are dangerous but common thoughts for many leaders. It's a mindset that silences the unique voices on your team. It crushes creativity, debate and growth. Instead, ask your teammates why they do things a certain way and how they think about and view things. If you know their perspective, you can better understand them. If you understand them, you learn to lead them better and value the contributions they bring.

Don't try to make those you lead into a version of you. Empower them to be the best version of themselves, to use their unique gifts every day. Be for your people.

Day 344

If you have a boss, you might be waiting on her to create a better culture for your team. She is the boss, after all. It's her responsibility. You're not wrong, but what if she doesn't? What if there are actions to be taken, behaviors to be modeled, and you do nothing? You can blame the boss, but that's not prohibiting you from taking action. No one is prohibiting you from leading those around you. You are inhibiting yourself.

There's also the opportunity to lead up, to impact your boss and to help create the culture you want, the culture you know is not only needed, but possible. It requires you to be the leader you are capable of being. To be bold, to be courageous, to go first.

Don't wait on anyone, even the boss, to create the culture. Lead where you are. Be the standard.

Day 345

Think back to yesterday, last week, last month. What successes did your team have? Not only in productivity, but the overall culture. What happened that reminded people of why they love to be there? What took place that people couldn't wait to tell their family, friends and industry peers about? What happened that you wish would happen on a regular basis?

Take note of the moments where those you lead seemed to be truly alive, both as individuals and as a team. Acknowledge them, celebrate them, repeat them.

Create a culture worth celebrating. A culture that people can't help but talk about. A culture people want to be a part of.

Day 346

When we're a part of an unhealthy culture we have a few options. We can complain. We can criticize. We can retreat into ourselves. We can quit. Those are the easy options. But do they fix anything?

It's easy to say, "This is bad, I don't want it, I'm out." It's harder, but far more worth it, to say, "This is bad. How can I make it better?"

To get a better culture, we have to create a better culture. We have to act. We have to be better today than we were yesterday, then be even better tomorrow. We have to show up intentionally. It's contagious.

Leaders worth following create the culture they want to be a part of. You don't need permission. Just act.

Day 347

Where there is fear, leaders worth following bring hope. Where there is uncertainty, leaders worth following bring clarity. Where there is tension, leaders worth following bring relief. Where there is drama, leaders worth following bring unity. They call people up to what they're capable of.

Leaders worth following are a force for good in the world. They show up intentionally, not accidentally.

Day 348

The world expects us to take the easy route. To care more about ourselves than others. To manage rather than lead. To quit when it's difficult. To not put in the time.

And the truth is, nobody would blame us. It's easy to talk about leadership but doing it? Very few want to put in that work. Everyone wants to be a leader. but not everyone wants to *be* a leader. It's risky, it's difficult, it's vulnerable. It's worth it.

The true colors of a leader are shown when the walk backs up the talk. Today, show up.

Day 349

If you ask the people on your team to list the attributes of the most impactful leader in their lives, there is a good chance their list will be full void of task-oriented attributes. Instead, their focus immediately turns to the relational aspect of that person's leadership. They'll say that the person pushed them to be their best in all areas of life. They'll most likely mention that the leader (coach, boss, teacher) was a great listener. They'll note how trustworthy and consistent the person was.

This matters to your leadership. We spend so much of our time focused on results and outcomes, finding ways to make our team be more productive. To be clear, we're certainly at work to do actual work. Rarely, though, does someone mention accomplishments when describing a leader who had an impact on them. We focus on the rings Vince Lombardi won but that's the last thing his players would discuss.

Leadership is about relationships. Your team needs to hear your vision, but it also needs to feel valued and known (and "valued and known" will look different for each person on your team).

While the world focuses on accomplishments, your team is more concerned about relationship. Lead for the good of your team.

Day 350

Life can be tiring. It can be frustrating. It can be defeating. We will have long, stressful days and we will have long, successful days. That's just the reality of the life we have.

As leaders, we're still called to fight for the highest good of those we lead. In the midst of chaos and stress and celebration, we must lead. We can't do that if we're not recharged. We have to step back and take moments for ourselves - even if it's just a 10 minute walk in the middle of the day. To fight for our team we must have the strength to do so. Your health, physically and mentally, must be a priority.

Leaders can't give what they don't possess. If you don't take care of yourself you cannot pour into your team.

Day 351

You can play into the fears of your team or you can pursue hope.

You can protect people from growing or you can challenge them to bloom.

You can plant seeds of insecurity and doubt or you can plant deep roots of encouragement.

Who you are for determines how you lead. Are you for yourself or are you for your team? If you lead for yourself, nobody will have a reason to follow you.

Your team is worth investing in, worth believing in, worth valuing. Lead like it.

Day 352

You don't need to have all of the ideas, all of the answers, all of the direction. If that's how your team operates, you don't have a team. You've unfortunately made it all about you, and others wait for you to speak before they move. You're leading from a place of pride and/or self-preservation. What's it like to be on the other side of you? Scary. Frustrating.

You're not a babysitter and you're not a dictator. You're a leader.

Leaders create an environment where everybody plays and is empowered to bring his best. That's when teams flourish.

Day 353

Mission statements are meaningless if you're not on a mission. A list of values for your team has no value if you aren't truly living them. All the rah rah speeches have no impact if you go back to normal two weeks later.

If you preach values, live values. If you preach character, live character. Leaders go first. Leaders define the culture.

Day 354

In every interaction today, check your intent. Ask whom you are really for in that situation. Are you trying to protect yourself? Are you trying to prop up your reputation? Or are you for the person across the table, seeking to empower her? When we're for ourselves, we go into situations looking for something in return. We seek out opportunities that can serve our needs, even if at times it is to the detriment of others.

When we're truly for others, we give without expecting. If it sounds counter to our always be selling culture, that's because it is. It should feel weird to operate that way. We're trained to fend for ourselves. Being for others is where real influence is built. It tells the person across from you that he actually matters as a human, not as an opportunity.

Leaders worth following are relational, not transactional. Be for others today.

Day 355

Leaders don't simply inform; they transform. They help those they lead believe and become more than they ever thought possible. Leadership cannot be conjured up, faked, summoned or copied. Though similar practices and principles may apply, leadership is unique to each leader. It must be real for it to bring impact.

At their core, leaders worth following are authentic. They empower others because they've been empowered. Lead with confidence in who you are today.

Day 356

A recent conversation reminded me of the arrogance I had early in my career. I had to be right, I had to be the winner, I had to be a big deal. Disagree or get in the way and I would do what I could to make you fail or feel small. It's humiliating, but it was my ugly reality.

The thing is, I was successful. Business was going well, which just fed my arrogance. Though, if I'm honest, that arrogance was a result of insecurity. It was a front I put up in hopes that nobody would see my fear and doubt.

I was successful, but I wasn't happy. Being all about yourself is exhausting and not fulfilling.

Everything changed when I made what I do about others. I made my work for the good of those I interacted with, rather than for the good of my ego. I sought to learn from others rather than force my views and agenda. I could be wrong and know that it didn't make me less credible. I became secure rather than insecure. Confident instead of arrogant. Now I not only had success, I had influence. Not influence that I schemed for or sought out. Influence that came solely through serving others.

Leading for ourselves is an fruitless pursuit. Our leadership and our influence come alive when we lead for the good of those around us.

Day 357

We live in a world where people crave the spotlight. They want to have a big platform (regardless of whether or not their credentials are worthy of a platform) and a lot of followers and for "important" people to respond to their tweets. They want to be influencers who interact with other influencers.

Leadership, though, is the opposite. Leadership isn't about you. It's about those on your team. About responding to their wants and needs and dreams. It's a "we" mindset, not an "I" mindset.

Influence comes through service, not a platform.

Leaders worth following don't want the spotlight. They seek to serve and empower their team, shining a light on those they lead.

Day 358

We tend to obsess with getting better at the task portion of our jobs. We want to be the best salesperson, graphic designer, IT Director, HR manager, coach. And for good reason, of course. This is, at a basic level, what we get paid to do. These hard skills can play a role in our career trajectory. They are worth investing in.

What if we were just as obsessed with being better at connecting with and empowering people? What if we took the time to truly know those we lead and understood how to lead them effectively? What if we knew what it looked like to challenge and support them as an individual, in order to help them be their best?

The call of a great leader is to help those she leads to realize and reach their potential. It starts with caring as much about your people as you do the tasks of the day.

Day 359

Power is the desire of an immature and insecure leader. It's the mark of a leader who wants control and who is unwilling to follow. Someone who is for himself. Secure leaders seek influence. They know they are at their best when they are empowering those around them.

Power manipulates, influence serves.

Leaders worth following don't crave power. They give it away.

Day 360

I'm not a caretaker. I love people, but my strength is in dreaming with them. Thinking about what could be for them, their family, their organization, their team. I see their potential and want to help them see it and achieve it. I see tomorrow, often missing today. It's how I'm wired.

When we had our third son, I noticed this play out - and, as a result, realized how stressful I made things on my wife with our first two boys. Recovering from a major surgery, she was limited in what she could do. I typically help around the house but it's on a different level when I'm having to carry the load of almost 2 people.

It would be easy for me to let things slide and say, "Hey, it's just how I am. We both know I'm not wired to noticed my surroundings. Deal with it." That's not what self-awareness is about. That's the sign of an immature leader.

Self-awareness is about embracing your natural strengths and tendencies but also learning when to operate out of a natural weakness. I'm having to intentionally to slow down and notice what needs to be done. To ask her what she needs.

To fight for her highest good means to step out of my natural comfort zone every now and then. The same is true for you and your team.

An immature leader ignores his weaknesses. A mature leader not only recognizes them, but knows when to operate out of them to turn them into a strength.

Day 361

Look around the office today. Look at the people you have the privilege of leading (regardless of title, you get to lead them). Listen to the conversations that are happening. Watch the way people interact with each other. Notice their commitment level to their work. Do you see people who might be hurting? People who need encouragement? People who need rewarded? Take stock of the culture in the room. This is the culture that is being multiplied. Is it what you want?

Be grateful for the opportunity to lead those around you. Own it, embrace it and be intentional in creating the culture they need and deserve.

Day 362

The need for control is a powerful thing. When that need drives us, we make questionable decisions. Everything is about keeping keep the control we have. We manipulate, we cover up, we avoid, we act out of character. We operate out of self-preservation. That fight for control will ultimately end in us losing control. It's a vicious cycle that leaves a wake of destruction in its path.

Instead of fighting to protect yourself, fight for those you lead. Let them be the heroes. Freely give what you've been given.

Insecure leaders fight for control, secure leaders empower others.

Day 363

It seems like most of the articles and books on leadership paint it as a sort of utopia. "If you just follow these three steps," your team buys into everything you say, you hit every goal and, on Friday afternoons, everyone sits around the conference room table singing "Kumbaya."

Let's be honest. Leadership is messy. It's dirty, difficult, frustrating, exhausting. It's also exciting, inspiring, life-giving, exhilarating, beautiful. Why? Because whether we are leading an organization, a team, a department, our family or a small group, we're dealing with people. Individuals with unique personalities, tendencies, passions, histories, fears, hopes and dreams.

And people change (including you). As a result, every day—if we're honest, every minute—is different. Every moment brings its unique set of challenges and opportunities. Ignoring this creates chaos and frustration, while accepting it enables you to be clear-minded in the midst of the chaos.

Acknowledge the messiness and the beauty of leadership. Lean in and embrace it. Welcome the story of each member of your team.

Day 364

Goals, resolutions, dreams. All great things, but they aren't enough. Everyone has goals, not everyone digs deep enough to determine the why behind them.

I'm going to lost 20 pounds this year.

Why?

I want to be be healthier.

Why?

I want to live longer/be around for my kids/etc.

Why?

My lack of taking care of myself has impacted my self-confidence, which is impacting my work and my relationships. My worth is not determined by my weight, but I'm hurting myself and others.

Now we're getting somewhere. Ask someone if they want to lose weight, and a good majority of people will say yes. Same with any number of resolutions people make this time of year. Including being a better leader. Why don't we do what we say we want? We don't address the root of the issue, that *why* we can remind ourselves of when we want to give up. We don't answer the question behind the question.

Don't just make a resolution or set a goal. Go further and define the why behind it. It's about the purpose, not the habit.

Day 365

Merriam Webster defines courage as, "mental or moral strength to venture, persevere, and withstand danger, fear, or difficulty."

As I look out across the landscape of our culture, something is missing. Something that is desperately needed. Where are the courageous leaders?

Courageous leaders acknowledge the reality of today while calling us to a better, more hopeful tomorrow.

Courageous leaders lead from a position of hope, not fear.

Courageous leaders seek to empower, not overpower.

Courageous leaders don't back down in the face of adversity, but push on toward what is right.

Courageous leaders don't give into gossip, criticism or naysayers; they stand on truth.

Courageous leaders are responsive, not resistant.

Courageous leaders know when to speak up and when to sit and listen.

Courageous leaders believe everyone matters, everyone gets to play, everyone is capable.

Courageous leaders don't divide; they unite.

Courageous leaders are secure, confident and humble.

Courageous leaders are liberators, not oppressors.

Courageous leaders are for others, not for themselves.

Courageous leaders don't bark orders; they fight alongside their people.

Courageous leaders have nothing to prove, nothing to lose, nothing to hide.

Courageous leaders fight for the highest possible good of those they lead.

Our schools, our businesses, our cities, our country and our world are desperate for courageous leaders. Who will step up? Who will answer the call?

What's next?

Thanks for spending this last year with me. I hope you have found yourself challenged and inspired, and that you are a better leader today than you were this time last year.

Now what? Leave a review. If this book had a significant impact on your life, I'd love for you to tell the world about it. Take 2 minutes and leave a review on Amazon. If you hated the book, you probably didn't make it this far anyway. I'd also love it if you emailed me about how the book impacted you. I love hearing your stories.

Give the book away! Who do you know that would benefit from this book? Share it with them, or buy them a copy.

Start over again! Really. You're a different person today than you were when you started the book, so why not go through it again to see how it speaks to you and challenges you in different ways.

Continue the inspiration by signing up for my daily emails here.

Check out the work we're doing at <u>Culture Wins Championships</u>, <u>GiANT Worldwide</u> and <u>Fieldhouse Media</u>. If I can help you or your team, I'd love to hear from you.